T0361573

Praise for *Anatomy of Desire*

"Dr. Emily is a master of sexual communication. She seamlessly weaves together scientific data and clinical expertise in an elegant yet accessible way and provides readers with practical tips and takeaways to level up their intimate lives."
—Justin Lehmiller, PhD, author of *Tell Me What You Want*

"Dr. Emily has broken new ground with her integration of 'flow' science and sexual teachings. Dr. Emily possesses a sharp mind, creative ability, warmth, and clinical expertise to move the client or student toward fulfillment of their erotic and sexual wellness potential. She exudes intellect, heart, and compassion with an upbeat flair."
—Patti Britton, PhD, author of *The Art of Sex Coaching*

"Dr. Emily's new book lets readers know that any couple can have an optimal sexual relationship. Everyone reading this book will find hope for their long-term erotic connection."
—Tammy Nelson, PhD, author of *Getting the Sex You Want*

"Dr. Emily is a new, unique voice in the sexology field. Her book moves away from the popular advice about spicing up your sex life and presents a fresh perspective on how to maintain eroticism in long-term relationships. Everyone will walk away from this book with clarity and purpose about how to cultivate higher levels of sexual satisfaction and enduring intimacy in their relationships."

—Barry McCarthy, PhD, coauthor of
Rekindling Desire

"Dr. Emily Jamea deftly weaves together clinical advice and stories with contemporary research, theory, and self-help exercises to give readers a well-informed resource for personal growth and sexual fulfillment."

—Wendy Maltz, LCSW, DST, author of
The Sexual Healing Journey

ANATOMY OF DESIRE

FIVE SECRETS
to Create Connection
and Cultivate Passion

DR. EMILY JAMEA

FLATIRON
BOOKS
NEW YORK

The author's extensive experiences and interactions with clients are used in the following pages. Out of respect for client confidentiality, all names and identifying information have been changed, whether or not so noted in the text. Furthermore, certain characters and client interactions have been compressed. The research participants provided their expressed written permission to use their stories when they signed their informed consent to participate in my studies. However, their names and identifying information have also been changed.

www.flatironbooks.com

Designed by Steven Seighman

Library of Congress Cataloging-in-Publication Data

Names: Jamea, Emily, author.
Title: Anatomy of desire : five secrets to create connection and
    cultivate passion / Dr. Emily Jamea.
Description: First edition. | New York, NY : Flatiron Books,
    [2024] | Includes bibliographical references and index.
Identifiers: LCCN 2024020670 | ISBN 9781250325402
    (hardcover) | ISBN 9781250325419 (ebook)
Subjects: LCSH: Sex. | Desire. | Intimacy (Psychology)
Classification: LCC HQ21 .J298 2024 | DDC 306.7—dc23/
    eng/20240615
LC record available at https://lccn.loc.gov/2024020670

Our books may be purchased in bulk for promotional, educational, or business use. Please contact your local bookseller or the Macmillan Corporate and Premium Sales Department at 1-800-221-7945, extension 5442, or by email at MacmillanSpecialMarkets@macmillan.com.

First Edition: 2024

10 9 8 7 6 5 4 3 2 1

To my family, for everything

CONTENTS

ANATOMY OF DESIRE

INTRODUCTION

Total absorption. Loss of space and time. Complete merger. These are all feelings that everyone wants to experience while making love.

This kind of sexual pleasure is an indulgence that can and should be enjoyed by everyone. And yet, my phone rings on a daily basis with calls from people who feel starved for emotional and physical intimacy. It's not just more frequent sex they long for; it's better-quality sex. It's not just better communication they want; it's a deeper, more fulfilling connection. Many of them have cycled through other therapists, and most have picked up some decent strategies along the way. Maybe they've reduced conflict, healed trauma, or improved communication, but they still feel like something is missing. I used to think that "thing" that couples longed for was a certain je ne sais quoi, a chemistry, that only some couples were lucky to find, let alone sustain for the long haul.

I have been a sex and relationship therapist for many years. Around the time I started having these deeper questions, I had gotten to a point in my career where I could help people recover from things like erectile dysfunction or difficulty with orgasm. I had helped women finally enjoy sex after years of tolerating painful intercourse. I had helped countless people recover from trauma, and I'd helped dozens of couples reconnect emotionally and sexually. But every now and then, I'd get a returning client who still wanted that something more—namely, or specifically, the passion like they felt in the early days of their relationship. When they'd lament about the honeymoon phase, I'd deliver my spiel about how the honeymoon phase gives us an intoxicating mix of hormones and neurochemicals designed for pair bonding. "If our brains continued at that level," I'd tell them, "we'd never get anything else done, because we'd be in bed all day long."

"Is this what we should expect forever?" they'd ask. I cited respected research about how "good enough" sex is something to be proud of in marriage. I told them how most couples in long-term relationships have what we'd classify as "great sex" only a fraction of the time.

Some would complain about wanting sex that felt like it appears to feel in the movies. I replied with my canned response about Hollywood sex—the thing we sex therapists are trained to say. "Those are Hollywood actors," I'd remind them. "There is a ton of prep and multiple takes that go into creating those scenes. Believe me, you don't want that."

But secretly, I knew what they meant. They wanted sex that felt free and fun. Passionate. They yearned for sex that made them feel totally absorbed, that made them briefly forget who they were while at the same time helping them discover new sides of themselves.

I started paying closer attention to the language my clients were using to describe the sex they wanted. Words like *effortless*, *absorbed*, and *electric* stood out. They wanted to feel *lost in the moment*, forgetting their woes and insecurities. I spent hours poring over client notes, going back through sessions in my head, and listening to people with the larger questions in mind: What were we all searching for in the erotic realm, and was it realistically possible to attain? And then it clicked. They wanted to experience a state of flow.

Flow is a term that was coined by psychologist Mihaly Csikszentmihalyi[1] (pronounced *chick-sent-me-high*). It describes the state of mind you reach when you're engaged in an activity in which you feel intense focus, loss of space and time, complete absorption, and a sense of unity. Think of your friend who is addicted to the runner's high, a jam band who plays unrehearsed music, or an athlete who gets "in the zone."

I'm sure you've experienced a state of sexual flow before: maybe during the excitement of a first time with a new partner or while on a romantic getaway with your beloved. You may have figured it was a fluke or assumed that sort of effortless pleasure can only come around once in a blue moon. But what if I told you that with the right mindset, a little intention, and a willing partner, it can actually be achieved quite often, well past the honeymoon phase? In this book, I share with you what I discovered during those hours of turning over my clients' questions: the five secrets to achieving emotional and erotic intimacy that stand the test of time. What is the key ingredient woven through each secret? You guessed it: flow.

Years ago, when I first became interested in the intersection of flow and sexual satisfaction, I turned to the academic literature to see what I could find, because I didn't remember learning about flow as it relates to sex during my studies and training. To my total shock, I came up completely blank. There was literally not a single paper that examined the relationship between flow and great sex, at least not among a diverse sample of couples. I found one paper[2] that looked at flow among couples who practice BDSM, but that was about it.

And so, I set out on a mission to get some answers. I initiated my own research study.[3] People could only qualify for my study if they were over the age of twenty-five and in a monogamous relationship for at least one year, because I wanted to rule out honeymoon-stage sex and sex that might be influenced by "new relationship energy" experienced by people in consensual nonmonogamous relationships. I excluded people who were pregnant or had a child under the age of one because, as any parent knows, that phase of life is not a very good reflection of the quality of your sex life. I then administered two questionnaires—a standard sexual satisfaction questionnaire and a flow state questionnaire. The sexual satisfaction questionnaire told me how satisfied couples were with their sex lives overall, and the flow state questionnaire told me whether they were experiencing qualities of flow during some of their better sexual encounters.

Sure enough, in support of my hypothesis, couples were more likely to be highly sexually satisfied if they experienced some elements of flow during sex. In fact, the statistical analysis showed that experiencing a flow state *predicted* great sex. What does this mean? That learning how to achieve a state of flow, which you are about to do, puts you on a new and exciting path of sexual fulfillment. The numbers alone were a huge win, but I wanted more. I called up the participants who got the highest scores and interviewed them to find out more about how they achieved flow during sex. Throughout the pages of this book, through their stories as well as other research and anecdotal evidence, I am going to share the secret link between sex and flow. I will illustrate how everyone can tap into innate qualities to cultivate the connection and passion we all long for. Shall we begin?

FLOW

Csikszentmihalyi outlined eight components of flow, which have been most notably linked to optimal performance in sports and the arts but can be applied to sex as well. The first component is **complete concentration**, meaning that whatever you are engaged in holds your full attention. The second is having **clear goals and immediate feedback**: you are clear about your purpose and know in the moment whether what you're doing is working toward or against your objectives. The third component is **transformation of time**, meaning time seems to slow down or speed up while you engage in this activity. Next is that the experience feels **autotelic**, or intrinsically rewarding. You're choosing to engage in the activity for the sheer joy of it as opposed to any external reason. The fifth component is **effortlessness**: whatever you're doing feels like it is happening totally naturally. Perhaps paradoxically, the sixth component is a **balance between challenge and skills**, meaning the challenge of what you're doing is just a hair outside your skill set, which helps hold your focus. The seventh component is a **merger between action and awareness**, which refers to a feeling of unity with whatever you're doing so that your sense of self and the activity become one. And lastly, there is a feeling of **control**, which gives you the confidence to fully surrender. That may sound like a lot, but don't worry—you don't have to check all eight components at the same time to experience flow.

Another principle to keep in mind is that flow is not reached by the flip of a switch. Instead, as flow researcher Steven Kotler describes, it happens as part of a series of stages.[4] Different from the components, these are the sequential steps one goes through in their journey to find flow. These are particularly important to keep in mind as you read this book, because one of the biggest mistakes my clients make is throwing in the towel too soon in the flow process. The patience of working through these stages is well worth it—and my five key secrets to great sex can help you move through these stages with more ease, understanding, and fun.

The first phase of flow is the learning phase, less desirably known as the *struggle phase*. In this stage, you're loading the brain with so much information that the body responds by releasing stress signals. This is why so many people give up at this stage. It can feel awkward and uncomfortable. Think of how you feel when you're trying to get in the mood for sex but don't feel it yet. You may experience distracting thoughts or struggle to connect to your body. It's frustrating! But people who trust the process eventually reach the second stage—the release phase. In this stage, your body and mind start to relax. In a sexual encounter, arousal may start to build as your mind quiets down. You start to feel connected to your partner as mutual pleasure builds, which motivates you to keep going. The third stage is flow: this is when the hard work pays off and you surrender to the pleasure of flow. A lot of people mistakenly assume that an orgasm is a necessary component of this phase. While it can be a part of it, and there is no doubt that an orgasm is the peak of pleasure for a lot of people, it is not a requirement to experience flow. For most people, an orgasm only lasts several seconds, but people may relish in the flow phase for much longer. Think about an extended make-out session in the early days of a relationship. You lost yourself (i.e., experienced flow) in the kiss alone. The final stage is recovery. This is when information is integrated in the mind and body. Your brain starts to categorize the experience into what worked and what didn't, what felt good and what felt uncomfortable. This stage will help you slip into flow more easily the next time you try.

I cannot overemphasize how important it is to be patient as you move through these stages. You have to be willing to go through a little bit of struggle and release before you can expect flow to kick in. What does that mean? It means giving sex the time, energy, and attention it deserves, just as you would any other meaningful activity.

THE FIVE SECRETS

Now that we've outlined flow—its components, how to pursue it, and some struggles you might encounter along the way—you are ready for a sneak peek into my five secrets for achieving it. As I organized my data, something occurred to me. Each secret is something we are born with. As you'll see in the pages of this book, we are all born **sensual,**

curious, adaptable, vulnerable, and with the ability to **attune**. But many of us go through experiences that disconnect us from these qualities. Furthermore, our culture and lifestyles threaten to strip us of these essential traits. The secrets are thus not about changing who we fundamentally are; they are about reconnecting with qualities that already exist within us.

In "The Indulgence of **Sensuality**," we will explore how becoming more embodied can take your sex life to the next level. We live in a very split-attention world and are more disconnected from our bodies than ever before. I'm going to teach you how to reinhabit your body so that you can more completely experience the sensual delights of sex. This is where we will explore the flow elements of *complete concentration* and *clear goals and immediate feedback*.

In "The Excitement of **Curiosity**," we'll discover how the power of an open mind enlivens your erotic life. You'll learn how challenging old beliefs and gently pushing yourself outside your comfort zone brings richness and passion to your relationship and sex life. This is where we will dive into one of the most reliable flow elements—*the challenge/skills ratio*.

"The Power of **Adaptability**" gives you the tools for maintaining sex that stands the test of time. Our lives are rarely stagnant. Couples who know how to maintain great sex have tools to adapt to new circumstances and evolving preferences, and it's well within your power too. This chapter illustrates how to make sex *autotelic*.

"The Intensity of **Vulnerability**" is about opening the heart. Here we'll learn how being in touch with our internal emotional experiences can add another intense dimension to our sex lives. It is only with healthy vulnerability that we can slip into the *paradox of control*, one of the most interesting flow elements.

"The Exhilaration of **Attunement**" ties everything together, giving you the tools to cultivate sex that feels effortless, in sync, and even transcendent. You'll learn the science behind anticipating each other's signals, much like a pair of ballroom dancers who appear to glide across the floor as one unit. In this chapter, we dive into the flow elements of *merger, effortlessness and ease,* and *transformation of time.*

Each chapter is devoted to one of these secrets. First, I'll explain the nature of each secret. Then I'll share my ideas on what threatens to disconnect us from each quality. And finally, I'll discuss how to reconnect with each component within yourself, your relationship, and your sex life. Interwoven in these descriptions are stories from my practice as a couples and sex therapist, as well as some stories about my own life.

One thing to keep in mind is that just as you don't need to hit all eight components of flow to experience it (some people only strike two or three at a time), you don't need to experience all five secrets simultaneously to have great sex. You may find that life has gotten too busy and you need to slow down, in which case you could focus more on sensuality. Alternatively, you may find sex has become too routine and you need to tap into curiosity. These secrets are there for you to dip in and out of when you find the spark has started to fade. You can think of the material in this book more as a menu than a road map.

I hope that as we move through both story and research,

you will feel in conversation with me and with your partner. Intimacy is vulnerable and messy and interactive, and I'd like to invite you to jot down notes in the margins, keep a notebook nearby, or perhaps share certain passages that feel particularly relevant with your partner. Opening up each secret on our journey to flow is something that can not only give us the deeply nourishing sex we want in our relationships but can also deepen our relationships outside the bedroom and enliven our own individual lives.

In this way, each chapter will explore a story of desire; not just a desire for sex but a longing to reconnect with eros. *Eros* is the root word for *erotic*, which we often associate with sex, but it means so much more. Plato conceived eros as "a fundamental creative impulse having a sensual element."[5] Freud used eros to describe our life-preserving instinct. In other words, it is the motivation to protect and express the body and mind. There is perhaps no more powerful or meaningful way to feel alive than to align with another person, mind, body, and soul, which is what I hope to illustrate to you over the next several chapters. In addition to client stories, you'll also get snippets of stories from my research participants. I am deeply indebted to both groups of people—to my clients for trusting me to guide them along their journeys and for their incredible courage to heal, and to my research participants who so eagerly and candidly shared their stories of love, sex, and desire.

Before we go any further, I'd like to say a few important things about the limits of my research and practice. The suggestions and guidance in this book are just that— suggestions. When you start to learn the anatomy of your own desire, you may find that some components fit while others don't. There is never a one-size-fits-all approach to emotional health, and this is especially true in the sexual sphere. People always ask me if the sex they are having is "normal." And my response is always that (as long as there is mutual consent) only they can determine what is normal and healthy for them. Furthermore, my words aren't a substitute for therapy. I find that the intimacy of couple's therapy can bring us into astonishing alignment with our partners and may pair nicely with the guidance in these pages. Additionally, I will be primarily (but not totally) using gendered language throughout the book, as I will be relaying the experiences of clients I have served, the majority of which are cisgendered and heterosexual, but the practice of getting to know ourselves and our bodies spans across all genders and sexualities. My practice also focuses on couples in long-term relationships, and my research and takeaways are tailored to this relationship structure as I've specifically looked into how to sustain a passionate connection with one primary partner outside of the honeymoon phase. Of course, great sex happens in all relationship structures, and I believe my tenets apply to a variety of relationship agreements. Finally, I'd like to add that the recommendations in this book may not be best suited to neurodivergent individuals or people recovering from recent significant trauma, mental health issues, or relationship betrayal, at least not as a first step in healing. There are many wonderful books on sex and relationships that cater to specific populations and circumstances, which I encourage you to explore before or in conjunction with the material in this book. For recommended reading and additional resources, visit www .anatomyofdesire.com.

You're going to meet several of my clients in the pages of this book, but I want to begin by telling you about Zoe and Mike, one of the first couples I treated after my research. They were in their early forties when they came to see me for help reviving passion in their marriage. Like most of the couples I'd counseled over the years, they described a hot-and-heavy honeymoon phase—a full year of total bliss. They couldn't keep their hands off each other. Sex felt totally spontaneous and effortless. Not only that, it was experimental and fun too.

Fast-forward fifteen years. Three kids. A mortgage. They were connected but disconnected. It had gotten to the point that they felt like two ships passing in the night, tag-teaming the kids' after-school activities. She'd do homework with one while he'd bathe another. They tried to do date night once a month, but they'd usually be so exhausted or full or tipsy afterward that they'd pass out as soon as they got home. If Zoe was in the mood, Mike wasn't. If Mike was in the mood, Zoe wasn't. Did the fact that she could count on one hand the number of times they'd had sex in the last year mean that they'd fallen out of love? Surely their marriage wasn't over. She was determined to get things back on track.

Which is how they came to find themselves sitting across from me at their first-ever therapy appointment. We dove in. We identified the things that were most likely contributing to the disconnect and started to work on them. As I worked with them to heal old wounds and deepen intimacy, things started to improve. They found themselves laughing together again. They went on vacation and had good sex. They reconnected not just physically but emotionally too. Satisfied with their progress, we decided to follow up two months later, just for accountability.

They returned.

"Emily," they said, "we're happy with our progress, but we want more. We want the kind of sex we used to have in the early days. We are having more frequent sex, and we feel more connected, but it's still missing that crazy chemistry we had in the honeymoon phase. Is it possible to get that back?"

This time, I didn't give my spiel about the honeymoon phase. I was armed with a different set of knowledge. I was overjoyed that through my research, I had discovered that the answer was an enthusiastic yes. The exhilaration I felt at being able to offer something more was mirrored in the excitement Mike and Zoe clearly felt hearing that "good enough" wasn't enough. I will never forget that feeling, knowing that we had another exciting step in the journey ahead of us. I hope that while we get to know each other over the course of these pages, we too share that moment of hope and excitement.

I continued to work with Zoe and Mike over the next several months. As I was doing my research, I counseled them on how to engage with the full potential of each of the five secrets I'm about to share with you. I am pleased to share that Zoe and Mike eventually tapped into exactly what you are about to: the full erotic potential that is written into our very DNA. There is so much beauty and intimacy and connection ahead. I am so excited to be with you on this journey of finding your flow and reaching erotic attunement with your partner.

1

THE INDULGENCE OF SENSUALITY

Silently the senses abandon their defenses.
—"Music of the Night" from *The Phantom of the Opera*

I first met Nina and Lucas, an impeccably dressed couple in their midforties, on a dreary February day. She was originally from Costa Rica, and he was from Sweden. One of the things I love most about practicing in Houston is how international my client base is. Houston has more nationalities represented than any other city in the United States. I've worked with people from all over the world, which brings such life, interest, and culture to my practice. Nina and Lucas had met fifteen years earlier in San Antonio. He was there for a business meeting, and she was staying at the same hotel with friends. Like many Houstonians, he worked in oil and gas, which meant he traveled a lot. At the time they met, he was living in San Francisco. They stayed in touch and eventually coordinated a few long-weekend visits together. The relationship grew, and before they knew it, he had put in for a transfer to Houston to be closer to her. Within a few months, they were married. In their time together as a couple, they'd lived in four different countries and had three children. They'd finally settled down in Houston again, where his main office was based, so that the kids could have more stability now that they were school-aged.

Today, they sat across from me in my office, clearly a bit uncomfortable.

"What brings you in?" I asked.

"We are disconnected romantically and sexually," Nina said. "We are generally disconnected. We love each other. We have a strong foundation in our relationship—it's not like we fight a lot. There is no abuse, alcoholism, or illness, nothing major like that. But I feel like the romance isn't there anymore, at least not like it was."

Lucas looked out the window before glancing at me and then down at his hands, which he was fiddling in his lap.

Nina continued, "We've had some amazing years together, but it hasn't always been easy. Lucas works a lot, obviously. We've had to relocate several times, adjust to new environments and new cultures. It's been fun for me, but I'm not sure he's felt the same. I feel like we've had these exciting opportunities to see the world, but for him, it may as well have been the same old office. I get out. I make friends with other moms. Having babies makes it easy to connect with women. But he's so focused on his career. I'm just not sure I even know what he enjoys anymore."

I turned to Lucas.

"I can't deny what she's saying," he said. "I love my wife. I love our children. I love our life. I do work a lot, but it's so I can provide a great life for my family. I come home every night. It's not like I'm out. But yeah, I can't say there is much passion. I just figured that's how things go. Doesn't that happen to most couples at this stage in life?"

"It can," I said. "But not to everybody. It's hard, though, when one person craves the passion and the other feels indifferent. Can you think of anything that brings you passion, pleasure, and excitement? What kinds of activities make you feel most 'in the zone'?" I looked at both of them, prompting them each to answer.

"Everything!" Nina exclaimed. "I grew up near Tamarindo. We were poor; we didn't have much, but we had the smell of the ocean air. We had music. We had delicious tropical fruit. We had an incredible community. I love to sing. I try—though not always successfully—to get the kids to sing, dance, and play music. I'm the one that brings life to the home."

"What about you, Lucas?"

Lucas went on to describe his own childhood.

"My family was upper-middle class, but my parents divorced. My parents got along well enough. They both happily remarried. I had stepbrothers and stepsisters. We lived just outside of Gothenburg. It's cold and rainy, but we were used to it. I used to row a lot when I lived there. There is a river that flows through the city. You asked what puts me in the zone. I'd say it used to be that. I'd get up early, right at dawn. It was peaceful there on the water at that time of day. I can recall the sound of my oars slicing through the surface of the water, through the quiet at that time of day. We usually spent a couple of weeks in Málaga during the summer, the heat and sun a nice contrast to the drizzle up north. Those were some of my happiest memories. But back to your question—when do I feel the most pleasure? I can't say I 'feel' it like she does. But I do enjoy the sex we have. It's not like we never do it, Nina."

Nina pursed her lips and looked at me. "Yes. We do it." She looked at him. "But I don't feel like you're super *into* it. It has gotten to the point that it just feels like we are going through the motions. It doesn't feel like we are 'making love.' I want him to savor me. Are my expectations unrealistic? Maybe, like he said, this is just what happens in marriage," she said sadly. She looked at him again. "It wasn't always passionless. I felt like you adored me in the beginning of our relationship."

I didn't think her expectations were unrealistic. And I don't think that people have to accept mediocre marital sex. Whenever I prompt feedback about desire and intimacy among my clientele and online community, I'm heartbroken by how many people are struggling with passion in their marriages. Even after fifteen-plus years of counseling people through the good and the bad, I'm still a hopeless (or, rather, hopeful) romantic. I ask people what they sacrifice in the name of love, and the answer is usually sex. How can two things that are so inextricably linked at the beginning of a relationship become so far removed? Sex and love go from being synonymous to estranged.

Nina was desperately trying to evoke passion from Lucas, but he, like many of my clients, had completely disconnected from himself. I looked at them. "I want you both to notice something. You, like most of my clients, keep using the word *passion*—and I get that—but I also want you to notice how when you describe passion, or being in the zone, you describe the sensual experience. Nina, you talked about the smell of the ocean air and the delicious tropical fruit. Lucas, you mentioned the sound of the oars hitting the water. Lucas, you are physically present, but not fully embodied."

I saw it start to sink in for them.

Lucas had done the "right" things—provided for his family, volunteered once a month at the kids' school, bought flowers for Nina every so often. He showed up. His life looked full, but it was diluted, a tall glass of room-temperature water, when what Nina craved was a frozen daiquiri on a hot summer's day. Nina was parched, but her thirst couldn't be quenched by what he was offering.

How had he become so disembodied? I wondered as I listened to their story.

WHAT IS SENSUALITY?

Sensuality, or embodiment, can best be described as the experience of relating to ourselves, one another, and the world through the five senses. This stands in contrast to "thinking" our way through life. There has been a movement in recent years toward more somatic therapy practices, meaning that therapists now understand the importance of the body (as opposed to thought patterns and behaviors alone) as a key tool in healing. People who are sensual and embodied experience greater pleasure in life because they are more fundamentally connected to the world around them. As it relates to sex, there has been too great a focus on "tips and tricks" that draw us away from the body. As we'll see, stripping away all the fluff and learning to reinhabit the body is one of the most powerful ways to ignite passion. The good news is that you already have everything you need to make the shift.

We are born sensual, completely embodied. We are

designed to understand ourselves and the world around us *through* our bodies, which are constantly receiving sensory input. When we were young, we were so fully immersed in our senses that it was the only way we understood the world. Our sense of touch is the first to form, developing while we are still in the womb. At just seven weeks, a fetus responds to touch on the lips and cheeks.[1] Before they have the use of language, babies and small children explore the world around them by relying solely on their senses. Newborns turn their heads to the sound of familiar voices they overheard while in the womb. Infants are instinctually drawn into the sweet aroma of their mothers' breast milk. Much to our constant worry, toddlers explore the world by putting just about everything they can get their little hands on into their mouths. Merely holding an object isn't enough; they need to taste it too. Babies' vision doesn't fully develop until later in infancy, and their ability to reason and think abstractly doesn't develop until many, many years down the road. For a long time, it's just the body.

While we don't have evidence to suggest that adults need touch to the lifesaving degree that babies do, it's hard to imagine that a life with minimal touch is healthy. The experience of touch is so important that without it, babies can die. Babies who do survive infancy without touch end up having higher cortisol levels and lower oxytocin and vasopressin levels as older children compared to their peers who were raised by loving parents.[2] I would go so far as to say that minimal touch in adulthood prevents us from fully thriving.

Every one of us, at one point in time, was fully capable of pure sensuality because that is how we made sense of the environment around us. Sensuality is an ability that is innate within all of us. And what's so beautiful about that is that we simply have to reconnect with what's already there as opposed to creating something that never existed before.

Unfortunately, our culture is quick to encourage a mind-body disconnect. "Use your head!" "Think before you act!" We start getting these messages at a very young age. The world is a deliciously vibrant place, but over time, as higher-order thinking in the brain takes over and our lives shift to the things we are "supposed" to be doing, we forget how to just be. We go from human *beings* to human *doings*. And spoiler alert—passion diminishes in the process. As a quick exercise, *think* about the last time you felt passionate about something. Identify the when/where/what. Now . . . try to reconnect with how passion *felt* in your body. Sit with those sensations for a minute. Notice how recalling the memory would have been different had I not followed up with a question about reconnecting with the sensations of passion in the body. I want us all to consider the extent to which we understand ourselves by our behaviors—doings—versus our innate being. Our being is comprised of thoughts, beliefs, values, and—to an extent—behaviors, but our *being*, our essence, all starts with the body.

Charging through a to-do list is so satisfying—I get it!—but consider how the satisfaction we feel from crossing things off a list compares to the enjoyment of savoring that first cup of coffee in the morning or lying on the beach enjoying the warmth of the sun on your face and the sound of the ocean gently lapping against the shore. Which moments are you more likely to remember—the day you accomplished your goals for the week or that perfect day at the beach?

Then there's the impact of the frustration we feel when we don't get every little goal accomplished. If I had a dollar for every client who lamented not being able to focus on sex because they felt distracted by everything else they needed to get done, I'd be rich. We center our worlds around what we *need* to do, instead of leaning into what we *want* to savor in life and what kind of human *being* we want to be. As entrepreneur Alex Gibb says in his TEDx Talk, we need to drop the to-do list and create a to-be list. When we're present in the moment, we are tuned in to and remember the way something *felt*.[3]

I must remind myself of this daily. Like many women after having kids, I found myself pulled between my career and children, between my husband and my friends. Life got hard. I was working on expanding my business as I was having my babies, and I wanted it all. The idea of slowing down or, God forbid, putting my career on hold freaked me out. I didn't feel like I could keep up with everything I was doing. I stayed up at night, my mind racing with everything that needed to get *done*.

Then I noticed something. Rather than feeling inspired by women who seemed to be doing it all, I found myself envious of women who found pockets of time to slow down. I had a friend who slipped away to a silent meditation retreat. I had another friend who forwent more financial gain to follow her passion for painting. I wished I had their guts. I realized then that what really takes guts is to break the mold. As someone once said, "You can have it all, just not all at once." I didn't want to live as another human doing. As much as it pained me to do so, I decided to put my expansion on hold. I didn't quit working completely, but I decided to postpone one of my career ambitions so that I could slow down and enjoy life with my tiny humans a little bit more. It was, for example, more pleasurable to breastfeed without also scrolling office real estate listings on my phone. I found that I could enjoy the experience more when I was totally connected to my body.

This is the power of embodiment. Embodiment expert Mark Walsh explains, "Rather than being aware *of* the body, become aware *as* the body."[4] I want you to keep this phrase in mind for the duration of this chapter. That minor change in preposition packs a major punch. Because if, like me, you live a typical twenty-first-century life, chances are you don't spend much time immersed in your body. And yet, our bodies are such a vital source of information, especially when we are discussing sex, not to mention *great* sex.

Throughout this chapter, I'll explain how to return to our bodies, particularly to our sense of touch (psst, it's easier than you think!). Some of us are more naturally able to do this, like Nina, but we can all learn to tap into sensuality and unlock this secret's link to erotic passion. I was determined to guide Lucas back in touch with his body in a way that would allow him to share the passion that Nina craved.

I opened this section with a quote from "Music of the Night," which is, in my opinion, one of the most beautiful songs ever composed. As the Phantom sings this haunting song, he seduces Christine, encouraging her to *savor each and every sensation* as she joins him in his unique world. The music leaves my arms prickly with chills every time I listen to it.

Many of the most epic love scenes are ones that depict sensuality in a way that makes us feel like we are right there experiencing it ourselves. While sensuality can be separate from sex (we can experience it in a wide variety of circumstances), it's also an essential component of it. Consider the following examples that despite not being overtly sexual still connect us with feelings of eros. Think of the pottery scene from *Ghost* when Patrick Swayze comes up behind Demi Moore as she's molding a vase on her pottery wheel. All we see are their hands intertwined, covered in wet clay, but it is still one of the most erotic moments in Hollywood history. We see the power of sensuality depicted in art and music as well. In Gustav Klimt's painting *The Kiss*, we see a man kissing a woman on the cheek while tenderly holding her head. She appears to melt into him, and anyone looking at this work of art experiences the sense of merger and sensual pleasure the two figures seem to be lost in.

The ability to ignite every nerve ending in a way that overwhelms the body with pleasure *and* evokes a deep sense of connection and passion isn't an indulgence that only exists in Hollywood; it can and should be enjoyed by everyone.

As Hungarian American psychologist Mihaly Csikszentmihalyi writes in his book *Flow,*

> *Everything the body can do is potentially enjoyable. Yet*
> *many people ignore this capacity, and use their physical*
> *equipment as little as possible, leaving its ability to provide*
> *flow unexploited. When left undeveloped, the senses*
> *give us chaotic information: an untrained body moves*
> *in random and clumsy ways, an insensitive eye presents*
> *ugly or uninteresting sights, the unmusical ear mainly*

hears jarring noises, the coarse palate knows only insipid tastes. If the functions of the body are left to atrophy, the quality of life becomes merely adequate, and for some even dismal. But if one takes control of what the body can do, and learns to impose order on physical sensations, entropy yields to a sense of enjoyable harmony in consciousness.[5]

So how did we go from being extraordinarily sensual creatures to feeling like sensually inexperienced adults over time? And what can we do to rediscover our bodies and our capacity for erotic pleasure? It starts with giving the mind an opportunity to quiet down and focus.

BARRIERS TO SENSUALITY

"I can't shut off my mind" is one of the most common complaints I get from my clients about why they struggle to focus on, let alone enjoy, sex. And it's a complaint that I hear more and more in recent years compared to when I first started working as a therapist. I decided to reach out to my first sex therapy supervisor, Dr. Ruth Sherman, to ask whether this was an issue she recalled from her decades as a sex therapist from the 1970s to 2008. I called Dr. Sherman specifically because she had retired from seeing clients just before social media and smartphones took over our lives. I kept my email short and sweet because I didn't want her response to be influenced by what I was already suspecting—that constant multitasking and interruptions were wreaking havoc on our ability to focus.[6] I simply asked her what she remembered clients saying regarding their struggle to focus during sex. I told her that my clients were constantly complaining about being unable to shut off their minds.

She called me a few days later. "I wanted to take some time to think about this, Emily. And I have to say, that in my 30+ years of running one of the busiest sex therapy practices in Houston, I honestly don't remember a single client complaining about the kind of thing you're describing. Yes, we had our 'orgasm-watchers' or our 'erection-watchers'"—meaning folks who were so preoccupied with whether they were going to get an erection or have an orgasm that they couldn't enjoy the moment-by-moment pleasures of sex. "I had plenty of people who couldn't relax into the experience because they had body image issues. But I don't remember people complaining of being unable to settle their minds. Not the way you describe. I really don't."

If you're over the age of thirty-five, you can probably remember a time when life seemed simpler and it was easier to focus. Now distraction is ubiquitous, and many of us struggle with it. Neuroscientist Adam Gazzaley writes in his book, *The Distracted Mind*, that "we seem to have lost the ability to single-task . . . We act as though we are no longer interested in or able to stay idle and simply do nothing . . . where we used to read, we now skim."[7] The idea of skimming stuck with me. I kept thinking how so many of my clients were telling stories that suggested they were skimming through sex: not fully present, not embracing the richness of each touch. Skimming, in many ways, seemed the opposite of embracing sensuality. No one looks forward to sitting down and skimming a good book. We look forward to luxuriating in rich prose, being transported to other worlds, enveloping ourselves in the story. No one looks forward to scarfing down fast food on the road. We look forward to savoring a delicious, well-prepared meal. We don't want to quickly plunge in the tub only to hop back out again. We anticipate the relaxation that comes with using bath salts and lighting candles. Why not approach sex the same way? My guess is that more of us skim through sex than we realize and that our increased levels of dissatisfaction, disconnection, and ultimately diminishing interest are because of it.

Multitasking not only wreaks havoc on our ability to focus but also significantly increases our overall stress levels. Our brains have not adapted to keeping up with the constant input of information they receive, particularly from technology. It's one thing to brush your teeth while you watch the morning news or call your mother while driving home from work, but quite another to, say, assemble a comprehensive marketing report at the same time you're fielding incoming emails from your boss. It's hard to play a complete game of Monopoly with your family while also paying attention to the podcast airing from the earbud discreetly embedded in your ear. The brain *can* handle more than one task at a time, particularly when those tasks aren't competing for the same cognitive resources, but it starts misfiring when we attempt to do two similar tasks at once and essentially fails if we try to add a third task.[8]

What happens when you've got dinner on the stove while trying to help your eleven-year-old with her math homework and simultaneously reviewing the Thanksgiving menu with your mother-in-law on the phone? You'll either overcook the chicken, your kid will turn in an incomplete assignment, or you'll neglect to bring the green bean casserole because you forgot to jot it down after your phone call.

One study found that office employees focus for an average of only eleven minutes before being interrupted by an email, phone call, or tap on the shoulder and that it takes an average of *twenty-five minutes* to regain focus on the task at hand.[9] Another study found that when email was taken away for five days, people multitasked less, focused longer on tasks, and had lower physical stress responses, as measured by heart rate variability.[10] If it takes twenty-five minutes to refocus on something as benign as an accounting spreadsheet, imagine how much more challenging it is to refocus on something as personal, intimate, and vulnerable as sex. Imagine you're trying to connect to your lover but the phone dings, the dog barks, or you suddenly remember you never called your sister back. The more we pack into our days, the more challenging it will be to center ourselves enough to fully enjoy erotic connection. Our lifestyles set us up for a slew of distractions. In other words, our lifestyles have become a total sexual buzzkill.

When was the last time you ate a complete meal without checking your phone? Do you focus on your body during exercise, or are you simultaneously listening to a podcast? How many minutes of uninterrupted time do you spend playing with your children? Are you guilty of replying to a text while stopped at a red light? Even when we're trying to relax in front of the television, many of us periodically check our phones at the same time. If you're like I used to be, you probably think it is relaxing to browse social media. Even though it feels like we're zoning out while swiping away, it actually activates the nervous system and sends stress signals throughout the body.[11] Ask yourself, if you multitask so much throughout the day, is it reasonable to think you'll be able to focus—really focus—during sex?

As technology evolves, we are training our brains to focus on many things at once, which makes it harder to focus on any one task when we want to. Think of yourself like a computer: the more browser tabs you have open, the slower your processing speed. Our distracted minds make it hard to pay attention to sexual cues, which in turn makes it harder to feel in sync with our partners. This inhibits our ability to immerse ourselves in the sensual pleasures of sex, even if we are still going through the motions. Furthermore, the increased stress response we experience because of multitasking makes it hard for us to relax enough at the end of the day to even get in the mood.[12]

So, what do we do? I find general mindfulness exercises to be a helpful first step for my clients. When intrusive thoughts or distractions occur, mindfulness teaches us to respond without judgment. This lessens the frustration we feel about distractions and helps us refocus on pleasure and sensation. But this isn't enough. Don't forget the research cited previously that highlights how long it takes workers to refocus on a task after being interrupted. Most people don't even have sex for as long as it would take to refocus on it after an interruption. We need to take it a step further. We need to start by minimizing the number of distractions coming in.

This begins with cultivating an uninterrupted life. When you work, focus on work. When you exercise, focus on your body. When you eat, savor your food. In other words, get back into your body the way you did as a child, before you had a million little fires to put out every single day, before life's modern-day demands got the best of you. See how you can carve out time in your life to reinhabit your body. Doing so will help your body function as it was meant to function. Sensuality outside the bedroom enhances sensuality inside the bedroom. As you are journeying back into your body, do so with a sense of openness, curiosity, and playfulness, just like a child would. If you take yourself too seriously, you won't have much fun with it.

DISCOVERING SENSUALITY
WITHIN YOURSELF

It was my second session with Lucas and Nina. I wanted to help Lucas better understand the parts of his life where he did feel embodied. I remembered him mentioning waking up early to row, and I wanted to know more.

"Lucas," I began, "tell me more about rowing. What do you remember about how that felt in your body?"

He exhaled and visibly relaxed as he began to describe it. "It's sensational. It's like the water and the boat become a part of your body. The little nuances in the water, the current, it communicates with you so that you know what to do . . . how to adjust your oar, which way to lean, how hard to pull before you even have the conscious thought. It's almost like your body moves automatically in response to the water, which is great because your brain quiets down."

"When was the last time you rowed?" I asked.

He laughed. "I'm sure it's been twenty years. I don't think I've rowed since I was at university."

I smiled at him. "Can you guess your homework?"

"You want me to row? I'm not sure what that has to do with sex."

"We've got to turn on the pleasure pathways in your brain and in your body. I think they've been asleep for a long time."

I explained how research shows that people who are more in touch with the senses outside the bedroom report greater levels of sexual satisfaction. I told him that it seemed he had been going through the motions of life for a long time and that this was reflected in how he expressed himself sexually.[13]

"Before giving you specific instructions for how to change things in bed, I want to focus on getting you back in touch with core parts of yourself—parts that have been lost but not forgotten."

I saw a flicker of hope in his eyes. Nina squeezed his hand and smiled.

My eagerness to get Lucas rowing again was informed by research studies I conducted in 2020 and 2021. In one of the studies, I examined the correlation between sensuality and curiosity outside the bedroom to sexual satisfaction inside the bedroom. In support of my hypothesis, I found that people who were more sensual in their daily lives enjoyed sex more than those who are more cerebral. The quantitative findings were a win, but I wanted to hear more about my participants' experiences. I took the participants who had the highest scores on the sexual satisfaction scale and followed up with open-ended interviews about what made sex great for them. They had plenty to say about being sensual outside the bedroom. One woman said, "I'm a sensual person. I love the smell right after a rain and my scented candles. I love tasting my food and petting my cats. I like to be surrounded by soft things—plush blankets, gauzy curtains. I'm physically expressive. I'm definitely a hugger."

Another gentleman said, "I love being in my body. I go to yoga two or three times per week. I love when I feel like all I am is my breath and movement. Don't tell my dermatologist, but I'm a total sun worshipper. I love lying out and letting the sun warm my skin. I love a good ice-cold plunge pool. It took me a long time to appreciate my body. I have terrible knees. I always have. I developed arthritis in them when I was in my early twenties. But when I'm having sensual experiences like these, it allows me to be present in my body without worrying about it. The aches and pains go away, and I feel pleasure instead. Funny how that can happen."

There are plenty of ways that we can learn to be more in touch with the senses in our everyday life. Doing so will help build pathways of pleasure that are more easily and more automatically reached while sharing our body with another person. Through embodied living, we can learn to flip on the switch in brain regions that have been dimmed. And with the lights turned on brighter, we'll begin to see, hear, feel, smell, and taste the world around us in a way that is transformational.

So, how do we go about getting back in touch with the five senses and living a fully embodied life? Practicing any of the following embodiment exercises will help get the ball rolling.

Body Scan and Illustration

Close your eyes and bring your attention to the different areas of your body, starting with your head and working downward. Notice how the sensations in each region differ, and try to identify what you're noticing. You may feel warmth and softness. Or perhaps you feel a sense of tightness like a rope constricting around you. Maybe a part of your body feels heavy. Maybe another area feels light and airy. Pay particular attention to your head, throat, chest, diaphragm, stomach, and pelvic region, as these areas tend to hold the most emotional energy.

Take this a step further and illustrate each area. (You don't have to be an artist!) Draw a rudimentary outline of the body, and then bring each region to life. What colors, shapes, symbols, and textures would you assign to each sensation?

Tuning into the body periodically throughout the day and identifying pleasant, pleasurable, and uncomfortable sensations makes it more intuitive to tune into and connect to the body during sex.

The Vocal Breath

Breath work is an excellent way of connecting more intimately with the body. Many of us are guilty of taking quick, shallow breaths throughout the day, maybe interrupted with a big yawn at best. While there are countless breathing techniques—and you should explore to find one that you like—I encourage people to start with a vocal breath. This exercise can be particularly beneficial after completing the Body Scan and Illustration.

Begin by taking a deep breath into whatever area of your body may need attention. As you inhale, imagine clean, oxygenated air traveling to a part of your body that feels tense or tight. As you exhale, do so with a loud, audible sigh. Don't be shy! Notice the vibrations of the exhale throughout your body. Draw your attention back to the part of your body that felt tense and notice what changed.

Another benefit to vocalizations like these? Studies suggest that people who pant, moan, and groan during sex are more sexually satisfied than people who stay quiet.[14] While you'll have to determine what feels authentic to you, it doesn't hurt to see how it feels to turn up the volume. Starting out with a vocal breath exercise is a gentle first step.

Embodied Movement

If you're like most folks, you spend a large percentage of your day sitting down behind a computer screen or wheel of the car. Maybe you exercise, but how often do you do so without simultaneously flipping through a playlist or running through your mental to-do list? The following types of movement are particularly beneficial for improving embodiment.

1. Yoga or tai chi
2. Dance
3. Swimming (bonus points if you skinny-dip)

Pay particular attention to the internal sensations of your body as it moves in space and the sensation of your body moving against the air or water.

Sensual Eating

There are few things in life that activate each sense simultaneously. Food and sex are two of them, so eating is always a good place to start. Choose a food or drink you enjoy and consider the following:

1. Begin by holding the food and examining it. Notice the subtle shifts in color. Examine the texture. Notice the little details on the surface of the food, feel the weight of it in your hand. Use your finger to feel the surface of the food and, like I described earlier, notice *as* your finger.

2. Bring the food to your nose and take in the smell. Notice the aromas as they come in through your nostrils, and notice what changes as they exit your nostrils. What effect did the warmth of your body temperature have on the aroma?

3. Hold the food near your ear. Notice what sounds it makes as you roll it through your fingers. Take a moment now and notice how your body is responding in anticipation of savoring the food.

4. Open your mouth and bite into the food. Notice the burst of flavor and the change in texture as your teeth breaks the food. Notice how it feels when your tongue swirls around the food and what it's like to swallow the first bite.

5. Close your eyes and notice how your whole body feels. Notice the pleasure you experience when you savor this food. Notice what emotions eating this food evokes and what it's like to eat sensually.

My guess is you're salivating just imagining this. Now, what if we replaced the word *food* with *body*? Just as we don't spend enough time enjoying the full experience of food, we don't savor our partners nearly enough. Just as you know when a piece of meat is ready to flip when the sizzle quiets, there is much to learn from the intensity of our partners' breathing or whether our touch evokes goose bumps on their skin. If you're not sold on the importance of foreplay yet, you will be now. Exercises like this will help you realize how much you rush through sex, ignoring all the sensual delights that encompass a complete erotic experience.

If you still find it hard to transition from connecting with food to connecting with the body, let's discover a few other ways we experience embodiment outside of our sexuality. Let's explore what happens when you engage in an experience that is truly awe-inspiring. Again, I don't think we do enough of this anymore. Think of our ancestors who gazed at the stars in wonder. Nature, especially big nature like tall forests, vast deserts, or anything with a panoramic view, offers a great opportunity to experience awe. You might even find that narrowing in on something simple like the petal of a flower inspires a sense of awe. Social psychologist Michelle "Lani" Shiota is a renowned researcher on the experience of awe. She has discovered that experiences that evoke awe and wonderment balance the nervous system in a way that, perhaps not surprisingly, also happens just after an orgasm.[15] It is in these unique circumstances when both sympathetic and parasympathetic activity drop at the same time. Think of how fully embodied you feel after an intense orgasm. Awe-inspiring events can have a similar effect and give you a preview of how powerful it would feel to experience that nervous system reset after making love. There are, of course, other ways to experience awe. You might feel it while experiencing an artistic work or by taking in an architectural wonder like the Taj Mahal. I know I experience it every time I attend the ballet. I am so spiritually and emotionally moved by this art form that it completely captivates me. I lose myself in it.

There are several ways that awe-inspiring experiences help us reinhabit our bodies. First, they give us perspective, which makes us feel small. This has the effect of quieting all the noise in our heads. Suddenly, our worries don't seem so worrisome, which is helpful because we can't live in our bodies when our heads are chattering away. Shiota points out that awe-inspiring experiences have the same effect as mindfulness, but while mindfulness takes a lot of work and focus, experiences that are awe-inspiring reset our bodies almost automatically, without requiring much effort. There is additional evidence that awe-inspiring experiences improve critical-thinking skills, make us more generous, increase humility, and make us feel more connected to others. Awe is a powerful emotion.

Awe, mindfulness, and embodiment all work together to impact our sensual experiences. Still, there are key differences. Let's look at the distinction between mindfulness and embodiment. Mindfulness involves awareness. When we practice mindfulness, we watch our thoughts without letting our emotions take over, creating detachment from certain destructive thoughts. This helps regulate the nervous system. When we live mindfully, we learn to mitigate the emotional reactions we have to our thoughts. Getting too emotionally pulled into thoughts activates our fight, flight, or freeze system dysregulating the nervous system. Mindfulness happens from the top down, and its effects are undeniably powerful. Dr. Lori Brotto, in her book, *Better Sex Through Mindfulness*, describes therapy intervention programs that help cancer survivors who report they "feel nothing" after going through cancer treatment to gradually rediscover pleasure in their bodies.[16] Traumatic events, especially ones that impact the body, can temporarily disconnect us from pleasure pathways, but research shows that mindfulness exercises help quiet parts of the brain that elicit negative emotional reactions and turn on parts of the brain associated with bodily awareness.

Embodiment, on the other hand, doesn't involve much cognitive function or effort. When we're embodied, we experience life more from the bottom up than from the top down. Our bodies can be a hidden source of intelligence if we learn to pay attention. As Dr. Peggy Kleinplatz, one of the leaders on optimal sex research, says in her book *Magnificent Sex*, "Both mindfulness and being present involve being in touch with the moment as it unfolds, but the former requires detachment while the latter requires total immersion. This is not to say that improving one's mindfulness skills might not be relevant for magnificent sex as far as being aware of and managing distractions. However, developing the capacity for this type of immersion and loss of self might be an entirely different skill, one that requires its own specific training and practice."[17] I agree. In my own practice, I've found mindfulness to be beneficial in helping clients move away from intrusive thoughts, and it certainly helps them begin the process of reconnecting with their bodies. But it's not enough for the clients to return to therapy unwilling to settle for "good enough" sex. Embodiment is what transforms sex from good to extraordinary.

My client Felicity, like many women, struggled to focus during sex. She felt bogged down by the never-ending to-do list running through her head, making it impossible to fully immerse herself in the experience. She'd just be getting into it when she'd remember, for example, that they were running low on eggs. She'd get frustrated, only to tune out for the rest of the experience, virtually extinguishing her own pleasure and that of her partner, who felt frustrated that she wasn't more present. Our early work together focused on mindfulness skills, which helped her notice the intrusive thoughts without letting them derail her experience. But like many of my clients, she wanted more. "It'd be great not to have to 'manage' anything during sex, including my thoughts. I do plenty of that all day long."

"Let's advance our work," I told her. "You're ready for phase two."

I explained embodiment and gave her some of the sensuality and embodiment exercises I described above. After several sessions, she had good news to report.

"I get it now," she said. "This whole time, it was thought-refocus-body-thought-refocus-body. It's like mental gymnastics while you're trying to make love. But last night, it was all body. I took extra time to get in touch with my body throughout the day. It's a little thing, but shaving my legs that morning helped me focus on the sensation of my smooth skin against my husband's hairy legs. I lit a candle. The soft light and pleasant scent helped me stay present. For the first time in a long time, I actually noticed the vocalizations of my husband as opposed to tuning them out against the pings going off in my head. I felt his vibrations as well as my own. I was embodied—not just mindful."

As we will discuss later, losing yourself in your body creates more cognitive bandwidth. Just as conversations at the dinner table flow more effortlessly when you're enjoying the meal *as* your body, so is mutual sexual pleasure enhanced when the mind goes quiet and the body turns on full force.

CREATING SENSUALITY IN YOUR RELATIONSHIP

How can you enhance sensuality in your relationship, and how will doing so enrich your sex life? So many of us live in constant states of heightened anxiety. It's become so "normal" that we don't even realize how cranked up we are. When we are in an anxious state, the sympathetic nervous system (the fight, flight, or freeze system) is always a little activated, which makes it hard to feel safe and connected—truly connected—to others. By learning to regulate the nervous system more effectively, *which can be done through conscious affectionate touch with your partner,* you can literally use your body to create profound connection.[18] While sharing experiences that engage each of the five senses is important for couples, this section will home in on the sense of touch, since that is the sense most commonly exchanged between romantic pairs.

Touch is so incredibly important, but sadly, it's not something we do enough of. Maybe you touch your kids or your dog all the time but fail to touch your partner on a daily basis. Touch can send all kinds of messages. Think about the message you get from friendly touch, like a handshake; affectionate touch, like a hug; therapeutic touch, like a massage or a luxurious shampoo at the salon; romantic or sensual touch from a kiss or intimate body caress; and, of course, the message you receive from erotic touch.

If you recall my research study I described earlier in this chapter, you'll remember that people who are more sensual outside the bedroom report greater levels of sexual satisfaction. When I spoke to my research participants in a follow-up study, many of them said they weren't just in touch with the senses as individuals; they were also very sensual with their partners and believed this helped enliven the sex they shared.

Julian, for example, described how sensuality plays out in his relationship with Bernadette. "I'd say my wife and I are both very sensual people. We spend lots of time cooking and gardening together. I cherish those moments of sensuality—for instance, when she leans over to taste a sauce I've got going on the stove. Just talking about it brings back all the senses—the dim lighting of the evening, the ruby-red wine that's breathing in the decanter, the aromas of whatever I'm cooking, jazz playing from the speaker. Of course, not every night is like this, but we have plenty of them, and sharing them helps keep us close, I think.

"She takes the lead in the garden, but I'm always there to help," he continued. "One day in particular comes to mind. We were both completely filthy, our hands and faces streaked with dirt and sweat. But we stepped back to admire what we'd planted and just shared the moment—the warmth of the sun, the fresh color in the flower bed. We went inside, feeling accomplished, and hopped in the shower together. Well, one thing led to another, and everything from that day led to such great sex afterward. The quality time, the shared sense of accomplishment, getting our hands dirty together. I took her straight from the shower to the bed, and we made love gently and slowly. She looked young, refreshed, and happy. I remember thinking her skin had a glow. I'm sure it was just from being in the sun, but I'd like to believe it was happiness and love."

Another research participant, Mabel, described the importance of touch in her relationship. "Being extra affectionate throughout the day helps build the tension for later that night. We are always affectionate with each other, but I turn up the heat on days that I want to have sex. I might french-kiss him before leaving for work instead of offering the usual peck, or massage his thigh when we're watching TV. These gestures send the signal that I'm interested, but also, it makes it easier to get into my body when we ultimately do have sex. I can't imagine being able to stay present and focused without all the little affectionate and playful touches we share prior to moving to the bedroom."

Katerina sheepishly confessed how she and her long-term boyfriend use movement to become embodied. "We sometimes dance naked in the living room. It's an unreal sensation, the feel of skin on skin as we are moving with the music. It's different from how it feels to cuddle or take a shower or make love. It's erotic, but playful too. The music, the movement, the absurdity of the whole thing. We start with giggles, but it doesn't take long for it to get serious. Something clicks. There is a look. Our bodies sync up, and yeah, one thing leads to another."

I want to share a passage from one of my favorite novels, *The History of Love* by Nicole Krauss. She writes:

> *Your hands remember a time when the division between the mind and body, brain and heart, what's inside and outside was so much less. It's not that we've forgotten the language of gestures entirely. The habit of moving our hands while we speak is left over from it. Holding hands, for example, is a way to remember how it feels to say nothing together. And at night, when it's too dark to see, we find it necessary to gesture on each other's bodies to make ourselves understood.*[19]

Not only can we learn a great deal from our bodies if we learn to listen to them; we can also use them as a way to communicate with our partners.

The kind of touch we received when we were growing up creates a blueprint for how our bodies respond to touch in adulthood, particularly in our romantic relationships. Take a moment to think back to your own childhood. Did your parents give you hugs and kisses, or were they more physically distant? Maybe you grew up in a home environment in which touch was unsafe or painful, as is the case with physical or sexual abuse.[20] Take a moment to tune in to your body. Imagine your partner touching you, and notice how your body responds. Do you relax? Do you tense up? Do you recoil? Do you feel warm or cold? How is this the same or different from what you experienced as a child? Safe touch from another person has the profound power to heal old wounds and restore your relationship with your body.

I treat a lot of folks who complain of a lack of physical touch in their current romantic relationship. A common defense from partners is, "I'm just not a touchy-feely person." While I do think there are individual differences in how much people enjoy touch, generally I argue that—and remember our theme here—we are all born with the predisposition to be touchy-feely people. As we discussed earlier in this chapter, infants can literally die if they are not touched at all.

I always ask my clients to describe what nonsexual touch is like in their relationships, and it was no different in my third session with Lucas and Nina. "Tell me what affectionate touch is like between you. Do you cuddle? Do you kiss before leaving for the day?" She gave him a look that said, *Be honest, mister.*

"I'm sure we could do a better job," he admitted.

"We could *definitely* do a better job," she interjected. "Although, Lucas, I will admit that since you've been rowing again, there has been an increase in physical affection. It's little things. You hug me longer when getting home from work." She looked at me proudly. "Instead of simply waving goodbye in the morning, he started kissing me on the mouth. He even spooned me before falling asleep the other night."

I smiled at them.

"Physical affection wasn't big in my family," Lucas said. "I don't think it comes as naturally to me as it does to her. I have been trying to be more intentional, and I'll admit it feels good." Highlighting that increased touch felt good showed he was noticing the positive benefit on his nervous system.

Let's talk about the nervous system, because that's the system that is activated, for better or worse, when we are touched. The nervous system is made of two branches: the sympathetic branch and the parasympathetic branch. If the sympathetic branch (our fight, flight, or freeze system) is activated by touch, chances are you'll recoil, tense up, and avoid touch when you can. If touch activates the parasympathetic branch, you'll relax, feel warm, and seek out more. Think of how you feel when a dear friend greets you with a hug versus your physical reaction when a creepy passenger gets too close on the bus. That's your body interpreting touch as good or bad.

The parasympathetic branch, at least to a large degree, has to be activated for us to cultivate connection and, ultimately, to become sexually aroused. As you can imagine, two zebras will not mate in front of a lion. So, if you're a person for whom physical touch evokes a state of sympathetic activity, you cannot expect to feel calm enough for sexual arousal to build. The good news is, with patience and intention, you have the power to reshape your nervous system so that touch evokes a feeling of relaxation and opens the gateway for romantic and sexual connection, as we'll see in the next section.

There is a little caveat here worth mentioning. Some people get turned on when their bodies are in a sympathetic state.[21] Sometimes the rush of something like conquering a roller coaster or scuba diving or skiing can turn people on. There are different ideas as to why this may be. A popular theory is a phenomenon known as *misattribution of arousal*.[22] When misattribution of arousal is at play, we displace the feelings of excitement during the heart-pumping activity onto our partners instead of crediting the original thrill. Make it out of the water without getting eaten by a shark, and suddenly, you want to devour your lover.

Then there are groups of people who see sex as an opportunity to soothe anxious feelings. Rough day at work? Nothing a good romp in the sheets can't ameliorate. And, of course, there are people who get turned on by risky sexual behavior. We'll talk more about the relationship between sexual risk and reward in the next chapter. As a general rule, though, the majority of people need to feel relaxed by touch to become aroused for sex.

Are you someone who struggles with touch? Don't forget that the brain is highly malleable. Through neuroplasticity, we have the power to break neural connections that inhibit our ability to connect and create new neural connections that open the pathways for embodied connection. Feeling skeptical? Let's look at the research.

There is a lot of evidence that supports the importance of physical touch in romantic relationships. Hugging and other forms of nonsexual touch cause your brain to release oxytocin, known as the *bonding hormone*. This stimulates the release of other feel-good hormones, such as dopamine and serotonin, while reducing stress hormones, such as cortisol and norepinephrine.[23]

A 2020 study examined the role of nonsexual touch in a sample of 180 opposite-sex couples.[24] The investigators found that, overall—and consistent with previous research—couples who touched each other more *and* who responded positively about being touched (in other words, they enjoyed being touched) tended to be more sexually satisfied and were happier in their relationships.

A 2021 study found a strong link between touch and general feelings of well-being.[25] What made this study interesting is that they found that touch had a positive effect on one's sense of well-being even among people who place a higher value on distance and autonomy. Why does this matter? Do you remember what I said earlier about how people come in saying they're "just not that touchy-feely"? Well, it turns out that touch is good for you even if you're someone who doesn't value it.

So, how can you rediscover touch in your relationship? I am a huge fan of rituals, whether they are small routines or bigger traditions. I encourage couples to create daily, weekly, monthly, and quarterly rituals. Pick a time each day for a mini-ritual that involves sensuality. That may mean a five-second hug in the morning before heading out the door or lingering in a kiss when reuniting every day. I know everyone has their personal comfy spot on opposite sides of the couch, but try in earnest to spend some time snuggling when you're watching television or relaxing in the evenings. Stefano, another one of my research participants, said, "My partner always spoons me before one of us finally repositions to get comfortable for sleep. We also snuggle when we wake up. We both love the warm, sleepy smell we have after a good night's rest. These five- to ten-minute snuggle sessions help me feel calm and deeply loved, a wonderful state to savor before ending and beginning the day."

On a weekly basis, try to touch longer. That may mean taking a bath or shower together, giving each other a massage, or sleeping naked. Skin-to-skin contact isn't just healthy for new babies but also has huge benefits between two adults. Next time you and your partner hug, place your palm on the back of their neck. When you kiss, gently touch the side of their cheek. When you're cuddling on the couch, wrap your legs around each other or use it as an opportunity to get a little foot rub. Try not to be covered from head to toe in clothes all the time when you're with each other. Spend time naked together even when you're not having sex. Skin-to-skin contact has the strongest effect, especially when it comes to the release of oxytocin.

We cannot expect ourselves and our partners to go from minimal touch on a day-to-day basis to mind-blowing sex. It's like trying to run a marathon when you've only walked around the block a few times. You've got to prime those pleasure pathways so they are ready for erotic connection.

On a quarterly basis, see what it's like to sit across from your partner in stillness and just be. I know this idea probably sounds awkward, but might I remind you that it probably isn't awkward to sit and stare lovingly at a new baby. As we get caught up in life, these behaviors grow fewer and may seem silly, but we are simply out of practice and further disconnected from our bodies. Take a snapshot of any random three minutes of your day. If you're like I am, it goes by in a flash—scurrying to get your kids out the door in time for school, racing to the gym to squeeze in a workout, picking up the dry cleaning while on mute for a Zoom meeting. Now imagine how wonderfully elongated three minutes would feel lying side by side with your partner, looking at them in the eyes while gently caressing their skin. That's where the magic happens. Eye contact with someone whom we trust helps us feel grounded, centered, and safe. Looking at someone who is grounded helps us feel grounded too. Look at your partner and notice the nuances in their face, feel the texture and temperature of their skin, lean in and breathe in their natural scent. Kiss and notice how they taste, really notice.

I assigned this exercise to Nina and Lucas. They returned the following week to talk about how it went.

Lucas began. "I haven't seen Nina in a long time. I mean obviously, I 'see' her every day, but I haven't really paid attention, you know?" He got quiet, and emotion filled his eyes. He put a hand over his heart. "I love her so much." He turned to her. "I love you so much. I'm sorry for just going through the motions over the past few years. Looking at you literally makes my heart swell."

She smiled. "Mine too."

Nina and Lucas completed this exercise after already having lowered the tension in their relationship and under my guidance, but how does touch fit into a relationship when you're experiencing conflict with your partner? You barely want to look at them, let alone touch them. A lot of people subscribe to the idea that the relationship must be in perfect condition for touch or sex to occur, but multiple studies have found that couples who engage in more regular physical touch handle conflict more effectively.[26] And as a therapist, whenever I'm working through a difficult conflict with a couple, I always encourage them to sit and face each other and take each other's hands as they talk in the therapy office. I find, and the research supports, that establishing physical connection makes the emotion flow more easily.[27]

Take my clients Keiko and Obe. They sat across from me in my office, each arguing their point about why they never had sex anymore. He didn't help out around the house enough. She didn't make him a priority the way she once had. I gave them a few minutes to reenact the fight they'd clearly had so many times before. When they reached a stopping point, I asked them to tune in to their bodies and describe what they were noticing. He noticed he was breaking into a sweat. She noticed that her face had become flushed with anger. Then I asked them to turn toward each other and take each other's hands. I instructed them to take a few deep, calming breaths and to look at each other for a moment. Then I told them to go ahead and express their frustrations once more. They did so, but with quieter tones and softer gazes. When I asked them to check in on their bodies again, Keiko confessed feeling like the tension had drained from her shoulders, and Obe admitted to feeling like the knot had loosened in his stomach. Without me even prompting them, Keiko became nostalgic, professing that she just wanted to feel loved and make love the way they once had. This one simple gesture—taking a calming breath, recentering the body, looking at each other, and holding hands—completely transformed the tone and direction of the conversation from one of adversarial debating to one of loving collaboration in the name of great sex.

CULTIVATING SENSUALITY IN EROTICISM

Now that you understand the benefit of embodiment for yourself and your relationship, let's explore how to transition everything to the bedroom. Not only does sensuality greatly enhance the sexual experience, embodiment elicits a state of flow.[28] According to Steven Kotler, embodiment is one of the reasons athletes have so much success getting into flow. It makes sense. People who have fully embodied sex often feel as though their bodies have a mind of their own, just like an athelete who is in the zone. One of Kleinplatz's research participants said, "A great sex experience for me is when that little soundtrack in my head completely goes away, and it's not a matter of should I move my hand here; my hand just goes there because that's where it's supposed to go."[29]

Embodiment ignites two wonderful elements of flow: *complete concentration* and *clear goals and immediate feedback*. The concentration piece may seem obvious. You're unlikely to experience sexual utopia when there is a baby crying in the next room or you're interrupted by the squeak of a dog toy that was buried in the covers. It's easier to concentrate on sex when you've applied some of the practices we discussed earlier. Put your phone away long before a sexual encounter, do what you can to minimize potential distractions, ground yourself, and create an environment that's conducive to relaxation and focus—dim lighting, a scented candle, freshly laundered sheets. Forget your to-do list. Set your intention.

It's relatively easy to make your immediate environment conducive to complete concentration, but it's more challenging to minimize internal distractions. You can clean up the room and wait until the children are sound asleep, but the mental load that many of us tend to carry is more likely to hang around. This includes things like planning what you're going to make for dinner the next week, making sure the kids have clothes that fit for the next season, and remembering you need to buy a gift for your niece's birthday. When my (typically) male clients complain that their (typically) female partners need every star aligned to have sex, this is the kind of thing they are referring to. They feel frustrated because (as any woman reading this can attest) the mental load never stops. There is always something. This is one of the reasons people like vacation sex so much more. It's not just the change in scenery; it's that you get a vacation from the thoughts that constantly occupy your mind.

In my work with clients, I try to move people away from the idea that we need to completely quiet the external (and internal) chaos before having sex. Instead, I show them how, by a simple reframe, they can see sex as an opportunity to escape their busy lives. The laundry will always be there, but if you're not careful, the sexual spark won't. This is one of the benefits of having sex that puts you in a flow state. Embodiment—sensuality—is one of the best triggers of flow. The state of flow itself makes it impossible to feel distracted by anything outside of your immediate focus. This is one of the many reasons why people seek out activities that put them in a state of flow—it helps them forget the world around them.

The second element—*clear goals and immediate feedback*—will also bolster concentration. Ninety-nine percent of sex therapists will tell you that you shouldn't have goal-oriented sex. Not me. I advise my clients to occasionally set goals for the sex they are having. What well-meaning clinicians are trying to say is that if you're focusing too much on goals like having an orgasm or sustaining an erection, you'll miss out on the moment-by-moment pleasures. This is good advice, but I also know that goals and planning can help us set clear expectations, which allows us to enjoy those smaller moments. In fact, the vast majority of Kleinplatz's research participants said that the best sex they had was sex they'd planned. (More on planned sex in chapter 3, "The Power of Adaptability"). Sometimes the goal is clear. *Today, I want to try to have multiple orgasms.* Sometimes they are more ambiguous, but there is a strong sense of what you hope to achieve. *Today, I want to feel like my partner's body is in sync with my own.*

It's okay if your goals are on the ambiguous side. In *Flow*, Csikszentmihalyi gives the example of a painter who may not have a clear picture in her head about how she wants the painting to look but will know it when it reveals itself. She knows immediately whether a brushstroke was working toward or against her goal. The same is true for a sexually experienced couple who intuitively knows whether their rhythm and technique is working in unison with the kind of sex they want to enjoy. It's easier to focus when you and your partner set goals for the kind of sex you want to have. Will tonight be an opportunity to experiment with power? Do you need extra TLC? Maybe tonight you ask your partner to focus more on your pleasure. Maybe the goal is a quick release, and you have "edge-of-the-bed sex," as one of my research participants described.

If it's hard to imagine how to start this process with your partner, you can begin with yourself. Feeling completely comfortable with your body while on your own is one of the greatest tools to feeling fully embodied with someone else. If you're a guy, chances are that masturbation is a more regular part of your life, perhaps something you've enjoyed from a young age. While the majority of women engage in self-pleasure from time to time, they tend to do so with less frequency and disinhibition than men.[30] The following exercise is designed to help you practice embodiment during self-pleasure. Chances are that you've discovered a masturbation style that works for you, and if so, that's great! Regardless, try applying the following principles to see if they enhance your experience.

Embodied Self-Pleasure

Relax ahead of time. Spend time doing what you need to do to calm your nervous system. Take a bath, set the mood, do some deep breathing or meditation. Minimize distractions.

Avoid visual stimuli. Avoid porn or other erotica.[31] Focus instead on the look, feel, and sound of your own body.

Avoid substances. Avoid alcohol and drugs, which will inhibit you from being fully present. You don't want to become dependent on alcohol or drugs to relax or lose your inhibition.

Don't go straight for the genitals. Instead, start by stroking your arms, legs, chest, and abdomen, remembering the mantra from earlier: *Don't just be aware* of *the body; be aware* as *the body.*

Explore the genitals. Touch yourself in ways you're not accustomed to just to experiment with how the body responds.

Remember, the mind-body disconnect didn't happen overnight, so the process of reconnecting isn't going to happen overnight either. Imagine you were a native Spanish speaker until the age of six before moving to the United States, where you learned to speak English. You may still hear some

Spanish at home, but now, at the age of twenty-five, you're most comfortable speaking in English. You decide to move to Argentina only to realize you need to brush up on your Spanish skills to improve your fluency. Is this possible? Absolutely! Will it happen overnight? Definitely not. The same is true for returning to your native mind-body language, if you will.

Anything that makes you feel fully alive, present, and focused takes preparation, practice, and commitment. Impatience is one of the biggest embodiment killers. Imagine a surfer who immediately gave up because they swam out with the expectation they'd ride the perfect wave within moments of paddling out or an artist who threw in the towel because they didn't mix the right shade of green for their landscape on their first attempt. They wouldn't do that! I say this to remind you to be patient, trust the process, and practice, practice, practice.

Giving ourselves time to connect with each of the five senses is one of the best ways to quiet the mind and reinhabit the body, which will make it more likely you'll stay focused during sex. Remember, you can't get into a flow state without focus and embodiment. I created an exercise called the Sensual Lover designed to help you slow down and connect with each of the five senses. You don't have to do each step in full every time you have sex, but I encourage couples to pull this exercise out when they feel they are in a sexual rut or struggling to focus during intimacy. What I love most about this exercise is that it not only connects you to each of the five senses, it also encourages you to use your whole body. If you're like most people, you're probably guilty of skipping straight to dessert. Sure, the genitals are packed with nerve endings, and most people require some genital stimulation to reach orgasm, but we have an entire body that's capable of experiencing pleasure![32] Not only will focusing on the rest of the body for a longer period of time help you transition from the craziness of your day into the erotic sphere, doing so also builds more sexual tension, opens you up to learn new erogenous zones, and facilitates arousal.

The Sensual Lover

Set aside ten to fifteen minutes for each step. Take turns being the giver and the receiver for each step.

You may choose to do each step a few times with increasing degrees of intensity. The first time, make it more like a massage, excluding breasts and genitals. As you feel more comfortable, you can repeat the step and include all parts of the body. Just remember that the goal is to heighten the *sensual* experience of sex. If sexual arousal or even an orgasm happens, that's okay; it's not that you're avoiding it, but don't think of it as a goal you're working toward either. The only goal here should be to heighten the senses.

For each step, talk ahead of time about any boundaries or limitations. This won't work if either of you feels apprehensive that your partner won't respect your boundaries.

1. **Touch:** For this first step, depending on your comfort level, use a blindfold, keep your eyes closed, or make the room very dark. This will help you both focus more completely on your sense of touch. Explore your partner's body, head to toe. Experiment with different kinds of touch. You may use your hands only, or you may choose to incorporate items of different textures or temperatures—a feather, candle wax, ice, a leather strap. Notice the vibrations of each other's bodies, the shiver, the warmth or coolness. Notice if your partner relaxes or if they tense up. This will also

give you the opportunity to start paying closer attention to their somatic cues.

2. **Taste and Smell:** Incorporate your favorite touches from step 1, but this time, also focus on the tastes and smells of your partner. You can choose to focus on each other's natural scents, or you can use essential oils, light a scented candle to help you stay present in the room, or even bring in some foods that excite you. Bite a strawberry out of your partner's mouth, or lick whipped cream off each other's bodies.*

3. **Hearing and Sight:** In this step, pay particular attention to your senses of hearing and sight. You may choose to create a playlist that you turn on as you explore each other's bodies. Or you can focus on each other's natural sounds—heartbeats, breath, moans. Whisper loving, complimentary, or even naughty words into your partner's ear. This is also your opportunity to really look at your partner. Notice the contours of their body, the pattern of freckles on their skin, or the way the candlelight bounces off their hair.

After you've finished one of the steps, be sure to talk! Discuss what you did or didn't like.

(*Don't use food or scented/flavored products on the genitals.)

The Sensual Lover exercise is wonderful if you struggle to slow down and connect to your body. The principles will feel automatic once you've applied them more intentionally several times using the guide above, and like my client describes below, you can incorporate them here and there to help keep sex exciting.

My client Camelia described the ways that her long-time partner played with her senses. "Once, when we took a shower together, he asked me to lie down on the tile and close my eyes. He played with the temperature of the water, first making it icy cold and then burning hot. I had no way of anticipating which way he was going to turn the temperature knob since my eyes were closed. The back-and-forth of the temperature combined with the anticipation and light power play was intensely erotic."

The sensation of pleasure mixed with pain is an interesting phenomenon. Most people think of the two happening on opposite ends of the spectrum, but there is more overlap than there is difference. While plenty of people are completely turned off by the idea of any pain interfering with pleasure, others eagerly seek it out. Think of your friend who orders the extra-hot curry or the exhilaration you feel when your lungs start to burn as you intensify the speed of your run.

My research participant George described his experience of pleasure and pain. "It's hard to describe the feeling I have when they spank me. Everything around me goes quiet except the sound of their hand on my ass. I'm completely absorbed with the sensations in my body. There is pain, there is pleasure. It's a total high."

A high indeed. There are plenty of neurochemicals at play

when it comes to pleasure and pain. Most people mistakenly think of dopamine as the pleasure chemical (and it is), but dopamine, along with natural opioids like endorphins and serotonin, is also released when we experience mild to moderate pain.[33] This may be the reason why exercise is one of the best medicines for anxiety and depression. The mild to moderate discomfort you experience when you push your body during exercise releases dopamine much in the same way a firm spank to the ass will. Context is important, of course. You've got to be into the spank.

Lucas had been working hard on spending more quality time with Nina. Rowing had put him back in touch with his own body and his own personal flow state. The increase in physical touch and affection had helped him discover Nina with a new set of eyes. They decided to celebrate their renewed relationship with a vacation. They returned a couple of weeks later to share their experience.

They were glowing. That's the only word to describe them. They were honestly radiant.

"God, we needed that," Lucas said. "I needed that."

Nina smiled broadly.

"Tell me everything," I said eagerly, leaning forward in my chair.

"It was incredible," he said. "Best sex of our lives. Better than the early days by a long shot. Being away eliminated distractions. Slowing down made it easier to connect. I didn't even realize how wound up I'd been until I wasn't. We took your advice and limited the number of poolside cocktails we enjoyed. I didn't want anything to take away from my experience with Nina. I felt like I was devouring her, and I didn't even realize how ravenous I'd been."

"Yep," she added nonchalantly, but with a flirtatious smile.

"I know we can't have vacations like that all the time, but I have faith the energy from that trip is going to infiltrate our sex at home for a while, and now I know what I need to do to turn up the heat when the flame starts to dwindle. I think I get it. I didn't know what I was missing."

Sensuality is one of the most basic skills you'll need to master to experience great sex. From a physiological standpoint, our bodies have yet to catch up with how we live our lives these days. Multitasking, tech overload, and general excess in every domain of life results in burnout, which makes it hard to quiet the mind and calm the body. But when you and your partner commit to finding ways to be more centered, grounded, and embodied, both as individuals and as a couple, you'll find that the energetic shift spills over into the erotic sphere. This will result in a sexual connection that, while temporarily making you forget who you are, ultimately leads to new, unimaginable discoveries both within yourself and in your partnership.

2

THE EXCITEMENT OF CURIOSITY

Who's to say what's impossible and can't be found.
—"Upside Down" by Jack Johnson

D id curiosity really kill the cat? My clients Naomi and Richard might have said so at one point—that is, until they learned to use it to their advantage.

Richard and Naomi entered my office and took a seat on opposite ends of the sofa. They appeared to be in their early forties. They sat in silence, looking disheveled. Their visible discomfort told me this behavior was likely out of the ordinary. The dark circles under their eyes and splotchy skin indicated that they hadn't gotten much sleep the night before. I could tell she'd mustered what little energy she had to apply lipstick before today's session. Richard cleared his throat, plucking off a dry cleaning tag that was still stapled to his trousers. She stared at me blankly, her eyes empty.

"I guess I'll begin," he said. "We are here because I cheated on Naomi. I was at a medical conference in San Diego last month. I ran into a woman I'd completed my residency with. We always flirted with each other back when we were in training, but she had a boyfriend at the time, so

I never pursued her. It started off with us catching up on old times over a drink, but we ended up kissing in the elevator as we went back to our rooms. I swear, that's as far as it went. I came home from the conference and vowed to put it behind me, writing it off as a onetime, selfish fluke, but the guilt was eating me alive. I blurted it out to Naomi when we were out for our evening walk with the dogs."

The air in the room felt thick, the only sound a leaf blower somewhere outside. Naomi couldn't look at him.

He turned to her. "I'm so sorry, Naomi. I would do anything to take it back. I want us to recover from this. I'll do whatever it takes."

I gently pumped my hands, gesturing to him to wait a moment. I looked at her.

"Naomi," I probed. "What was your first reaction when he confessed what he'd done?"

"Total shock," she said. "I'm still just completely shocked. I thought we had the kind of relationship, the kind of life, that people dream about. I thought we were solid. I can't make sense of this. Richard has a demanding schedule, but he comes home every night. He spends time with me and the kids. We still have sex. I think we're still attracted to each other. He's honestly the last person I would have imagined would do something like this."

"I can't deny what she's saying," Richard agreed. "It came as a shock to me too. The whole thing felt surreal, almost out of body. I can't make sense of it. I ask myself why, and I come up blank."

Naomi looked at him, a tiny spark of compassion in her eyes. I could tell she believed that this behavior, the choice he made, was completely out of character for him.

"People transgress for all kinds of reasons," I explained. "A lot of times, it's because the opportunity presents itself. Sometimes people seek it out. Sometimes it happens because of conflict in the primary relationship, sometimes not. Humans are complex."

"But Naomi and I aren't complex. She's right. We are living the dream. We've been incredibly fortunate. I've had career success. We have three healthy children. We take vacations together. We have a safe, comfortable home."

"You're giving me the Instagram version of your life," I told him. "What's below the surface? Tell me more about your relationship with each other. How did you meet? How did things evolve?"

Naomi cleared her throat, straightening up. "We met at a happy hour. Richard was finishing up his residency at the time. I was working as a drug rep. The pharmaceutical company I worked for organized a get-together, and he was there. He didn't look much different from how he looks now." She gently smiled. "Tired. He'd come off a long shift at the hospital and was still in his scrubs. I remember thinking it felt easy to talk to him. He asked for my number. I didn't expect much. Doctors have a reputation for having flings with drug reps. But he called the next day. He asked me out, and the rest is history."

Richard picked up where she left off. "We dated for a couple of years before getting engaged. Naomi got pregnant a year later, and we decided she would stay home with the baby. She had to travel a lot as a drug rep, and that seemed like it would complicate things once we had kids. We had our second kiddo two years later and the third two years after that."

"That's interesting," I said. "Earlier, you made a point of saying that you and Naomi are not complex. And just now you said that she quit working because her job would complicate life with kids. I get that, but I'm also curious—what is your relationship with complexity?" I gently pushed.

"I'm not sure I've ever thought about that," Richard said. "I just figure, life is hard. At least it can be. Simplify where and when you can. It makes things easier."

"And what about you, Naomi?" I asked.

"I agree with Richard," she said. "I'm a no-drama kind of gal. What you see is what you get. We've always been so transparent with each other. I honestly can't think of anything I did that led him to cheat. I'm emotionally available. I'm sexually available."

"I've told her a thousand times that this has nothing to do with her. I'm an asshole. I think it's what you said before about the opportunity just presenting itself. I'm not usually impulsive like that, but I have no other explanation. Maybe I was just curious about how it would feel to kiss someone else. Naomi and I have been together a long time, and I didn't date much before her because I was also so focused on academics. I don't know."

Was that it? I thought as I listened to their story. *Curiosity meets opportunity meets impulsivity?* I didn't think so. Yes, curiosity was at play, but it wasn't as superficial as he assumed. From what I could gather, they'd become disengaged—no longer curious—in an effort to simplify their lives. Lots of relationships fall victim to monotony, but theirs had become almost superficial. They showed up for each other—they did the things they were expected to do—but passion had fallen flat. There was something deeper going on, and I was determined to get to the bottom of it. I sensed that not only had their curiosity toward each other diminished, they had also whittled away parts of themselves in the name of keeping life simple. I put a star next to my note about Richard not having much experience before Naomi. Was this a matter of him having never sown his wild oats? We needed to reawaken something in their relationship. I decided to start by exploring curiosity. Would it kill them, or would it set them free?

WHAT IS CURIOSITY?

Curiosity has been defined as recognizing, embracing, and seeking out knowledge and new experiences.[1] That knowledge can be about the world around you or, more importantly, yourself and your relationships with others. The mere fact that Naomi and Richard sat in my office showed that they were curious about why this had happened in their relationship. Richard may have cheated because he was curious about someone else, but he was also interested in understanding himself as he sat across from me. There was also curiosity from Naomi about how in the world their relationship had come to this.

Curiosity can be beneficial in that it leads to clarity as you learn new things about yourself and who you are. If we simply accept who we are without considering why we think and feel in the ways that we do, parts of our selves begin to fade, which can inhibit personal growth. This principle applies to sex as well. When we reduce sex to a mere function of the body, we miss out on the important role that an open mind plays in expanding our erotic consciousness and awakening us in a way that is only possible for humans. We talked about reinhabiting the body in the last chapter, and now we are going to talk about how to open the mind.

Human beings are naturally, innately curious creatures. From the time they are able, babies enthusiastically explore the world around them. They look around, touch, taste, crawl, and climb. Curiosity researchers Jon Cohen and Spencer Harrison point out that four-year-olds ask an average of three hundred questions per day.[2] Their questions are interesting, provocative, and engaging. Middle schoolers, on the other hand, only ask an average of two questions per day, and their questions usually fall somewhere along the lines of *Is this going to be on the test?* and *Can I go to the bathroom?* We are all born curious, but our curiosity quickly diminishes over time as we succumb to societal pressures and narrow educational institutions. Much like we discussed in the last chapter with touch, I want to teach you how to reconnect with your innate curiosity. I will illustrate how doing so can help you optimize yourself, your relationships, and ultimately, your sexual experiences.

Why does curiosity matter? Curiosity is an adaptive quality that evolved to keep us alive.[3] It is an important precursor to motivation, exploration, and willingness to engage with new things. Animals who are curious and courageous enough to explore have a better chance of adapting to new environments, finding food, and connecting with new mates.[4] The same goes for humans. Curiosity is suspected to play a role in the development of meaning in life, ability to tolerate distress, wisdom, intelligence, happiness, and having engaging and satisfying social relationships.[5] Curious people, the research shows, are more likely to persist until they meet their goals, and they also process new information at a deeper level compared to those who take things at face value.[6] There is a link between curiosity and innovation and problem-solving. Being curious keeps you feeling alive, vibrant, and dynamic. The more alive we feel, the more intense our sexual pleasure. We also know that the more curious we are outside the bedroom, the higher our sexual satisfaction inside the bedroom.[7]

You may be wondering how this exploration of curiosity complements our discussion around sensuality and embodiment. One is about opening the mind while the other is about staying present in the body. How can they exist together without contradicting each other? The mind and body are far from separate entities. The mind is part of the body in that it is responsible for regulating the flow of energy between the body, the brain, our relationships with others, and our environment. Let me break that down for you. About thirty years ago, Dr. Dan Siegel sat down with a group of scientists across an array of disciplines with the goal of defining the mind. They decided that the best definition is *the embodied and relational emergent self-organizing process that's regulating the flow of energy and information.*[8] Without the mind, he posits, the harmonious flow of energy is blocked, and we fall into chaos or rigidity, which collapses the system. In other words, the mind, which is what I am talking about when I explain curiosity, balances the body alongside our partners within our environment. This sets us up to be more embodied, expanding both our mental and physical worlds. As we'll see in the next section, however, this expansion may be easier said than done.

BARRIERS TO CURIOSITY

For centuries, people in power have told us how to think, what to feel, and how to behave. Order simplifies life and makes people easier to manage. If you can predict someone's life and shape their sense of self, they are easier to control. Furthermore, humans have a profound need for acceptance and belonging. We are inclined to follow the rules because it makes it easier to fit in, and many would argue that life is simpler if you adhere to societal norms. Look at Naomi and Richard. They were very clear about cultivating an easy-to-manage life.

That's not to say that rules and expectations are all bad or that there is always malevolence from the people who make them. We can, after all, gather wisdom from people who have more experience than we do, but where is the line? What is the effect of our leaders, clergy, parents, and educators gradual shaping of our minds? What happens when we lose our sense of self, our individuality, our personal sense of purpose and become another sheep in the flock? I thought about this in preparation for my next session with Richard. I wanted to spend some time digging into his history to see what parts of himself he'd started to neglect. In an effort to make his life easy, had he become another sheep in the flock too?

Richard returned to my office the next week, alone this time. I always like to see my clients individually so that I can explore without censorship in the presence of their partners. Richard felt ready to gain more insight about how and why everything happened.

"I've been thinking more about what you said last time,"

Richard began, "that we gave you the Instagram version of our life. That was hard to hear, but it resonated. I've busted my ass to build this life, and it's a life I'm proud of. But yeah, it does sometimes feel like we are on autopilot."

"Tell me more about your life's trajectory. What made you interested in medicine?"

"I was destined to be a physician. My grandfather and my father were both physicians. It's in my blood. My older brother had no interest, so it was up to me to carry on the family tradition. I love my work. I enjoy helping people, and it's a great, stable income."

"What else did you enjoy growing up?"

"I loved building things. I had drawers and drawers filled with LEGOs. Math and science come easily to me. I thought about engineering but didn't want to break the family tradition."

"What about Naomi? Who was she before marrying you and having kids?"

"She was so many things! Did she tell you she started law school before quitting to become a drug rep? She has a brilliant mind. She's also very creative. She used to paint. Many of the pieces we have in our home are things she created. She's also a beautiful pianist. I know she wishes she had more time to paint and play the piano now, but it's hard to find time with the kids. I think she scratches her creative itch with interior design. She's made a beautiful home for us and is a devoted mother."

"What comes up as you describe you and Naomi before kids, before hopping on the train that was waiting at the station?"

"I think I get where you're going," he said. "But this

happens for everybody, right? I don't see what it has to do with me cheating."

I paused, hesitant to say what I was thinking, because I knew I was at risk of making Richard defensive.

"I wonder if, at least in part, this kiss in the elevator was an act of rebellion from what was expected of you and the monotony of your relationship. You've been on the straight and narrow your whole life."

"Okay . . ." he said defensively, suspiciously. "So I'm supposed to go back and tell my wife that the reason I kissed someone else was in part because she became a dedicated mother and I a respectable surgeon, the very things we agreed on and that we take so much pride in? She'll divorce me on the spot! I can't imagine how hurtful that would be to hear."

I took a deep breath, hoping it would invite him to do the same. "No, I wouldn't say that to her. And I'm not at all suggesting she go back to work or that you give up medicine. But I wonder how you'd both feel if she created time to do something that she's passionate about outside the home, something that's just for her. Painting is a wonderful way to express oneself. My hunch is that her sense of self and purpose narrowed since becoming a mother, as it does for many women. Neither of you need to make major changes to your life to discover parts of yourself that are lost. But you need to be curious about what you want that is separate from what you're 'supposed' to do."

I reminded Richard that it's impossible to separate your sexuality from your individuality (a concept you'll find more than once in this book—it's an important message!). Anything that makes you who you are is going to reflect itself in the erotic realm. The more facets a diamond has, the more brilliantly it shines. Richard and Naomi had both unwittingly whittled away vital parts of themselves, and it was no wonder that passion and excitement had faded even though they were still having regular sex.

While speaking with Richard, I was reminded of Elizabeth Gilbert's famous memoir *Eat, Pray, Love*, which largely revolves around her powerful realization that she no longer wanted a role in the life she thought she wanted to build: "I had actively participated in every moment of the creation of this life—so why did I feel like none of it resembled me?"[9] Like Richard and Naomi, she'd succumbed to creating the life she thought she was supposed to create but had lost herself somewhere along the way. I wonder what would have happened if rather than leaving her husband to rediscover herself (Gilbert divorced her husband and traveled around the world to rediscover her sense of purpose), she had turned toward him. What would have happened if her husband could hold space for the complexity of her emotions and work jointly with her in making adjustments to their life so that they both felt more whole? When it comes to coupledom, emotional and relational curiosity are necessary if you want to stay vibrant and strong.

It's easy to become complacent when you enter into a partnership, especially one that looks perfect on paper: doctor husband, stay-at-home wife, three healthy children, regular vacations. But you must keep talking, keep learning about each other, and discovering new things about yourself. This curiosity should manifest in a number of different ways: partners should be curious about each other, but also about themselves. Perhaps, for example, if Naomi and Richard had remained curious about their relationship and had more regular check-ins about their wants and needs, they would have been able to detect Richard's feelings of dissatisfaction with his preplanned life path earlier and discussed it in a more productive way. A couple is made not of one rigid relationship unit with clearly defined roles but rather of two individuals who feel whole unto themselves and who thrive in the relationship, rather than feel trapped by its confines. Consistent, judgment-free curiosity (and a secure attachment, which we will learn about in chapter 4, "The Intensity of Vulnerability") is the key that allows people to not only feel fulfilled in relationships but also free within them.

There are so many institutions that we blindly enter without questioning whether they are really the right fit for us. The choice to get married and have children is perhaps the most widespread. It saddens me how many people sacrifice integral, vital parts of themselves for the sake of love. It makes me think our definition of love has become distorted or, at best, diluted. Isn't love supposed to expand, not inhibit? Does love have to be synonymous with sacrifice? What would happen if we stayed curious and connected to all parts of ourselves *and* had a partner who supported us in staying whole?

Many of us decide to marry or practice monogamy or become a parent without asking ourselves why or whether these decisions are right for us. This isn't to say that they aren't right for us, but examining *why* they are or aren't is an important first step. Making well-informed decisions empowers us as individuals and ultimately strengthens our relationships. Ask yourself—to what degree did you curate your life versus allow life to curate you? It is important to stay curious not just at the time decisions are made but through the course of your life as well. You must consider how any decision you make will affect your sense of self, because at the end of the day, anything that affects your sense of self is going to affect the way you express yourself sexually.

Going against the grain can be scary. People are persecuted for blazing their own trail. Women notoriously feel "mom guilt" for doing things for themselves. Telling a long-time partner that you've shifted in the way you see things can be terrifying. What if they reject you? What if you reject them? Or, what if, instead of rejecting each other, you grow together?

Many of my research participants said that disentangling old belief systems was a part of their therapeutic, relationship, and sexual growth. Malone, for instance, described what letting go of destructive religious beliefs was like for her. "My whole life, I thought masturbation was a sin. I remember being a teenager and having intense longings to touch myself but fearing I'd go to hell if I did. You'd think I'd feel relieved once I got married and my husband could touch me there, but I didn't. It felt like my body didn't belong to me. I'd been taught my whole life that it either belonged to God or to my husband. I had no sense of sexual self that wasn't in the hands of another person. My husband and I found guidance from a spiritual leader within our new church. She gave me a new perspective on things. She explained that sex wasn't just for my husband but that pleasure was meant for me too. I realized that the church I'd grown up in, like many churches, cherry-picked things from the Bible that they wanted us to adhere to. It took a long time from learning that truth to feeling free from it. I'm lucky to have such a patient, supportive husband. I couldn't have fathomed sex could be this wonderful, this liberating."

How beautiful it is to jointly challenge culturally ingrained beliefs alongside your partner. Curiosity about oneself by yourself can be scary, but getting curious alongside your partner is not only exciting but also cultivates intimacy.

This idea of *unlearning* was also a theme in Dr. Peggy Kleinplatz's research.[10] She writes that many of her participants compare "their sexual desires to mainstream standards, finding these standards to be lacking or limiting or simply irrelevant to them and choosing instead to pursue authentic desires." This shift can't happen without curiosity about alternatives. I've worked with countless individuals who had to release negative, and at times even abusive, messages about sexuality before gaining clarity on their sexual value systems. What does it take to get curious about your own value systems, and how can doing so deepen intimacy and enhance your sex life? Let's explore how to cultivate curiosity within yourself first.

DISCOVERING CURIOSITY WITHIN YOURSELF

How can you foster your own sense of curiosity? There are the obvious things like signing up for a new class, listening to interesting podcasts, or reading books in subject matters that you know nothing about. Another way to foster your curiosity is to simply talk to people who have different perspectives. It's easy to sign up for a class, but it's not always so easy to find someone who has a completely different philosophy or belief system from yours. Especially these days, with the world being so politically divided, we tend to socialize only with people who share our same opinions and values and philosophies. We've stopped talking with people who think differently from us. Talking with new people isn't about changing your mind but rather opening your mind to new perspectives. In doing so, you'll understand yourself at a deeper level.

Travel is a fantastic way to wake up your curious parts. Anyone who's traveled off the beaten path can attest to this. I particularly love going to places where the culture is completely different from my culture here in the United States. It gives me the opportunity to immerse myself in a new way of life. In doing so, I take home with me something that expands my personality. Cultural immersion opens my mind in a way that keeps me feeling connected to all parts of myself.

But what if I'm not a curious person? you might be wondering. It's the age-old nature-versus-nurture debate that we touched on when discussing sensuality: How much of ourselves is fixed and how much can we change?

Aristotle philosophized that we are a tabula rasa (blank slate), believing that rather than our personality being determined by our genetic makeup, we are instead shaped by the environment and people around us. These days, most personality and behavioral scientists believe that a combination is at play. We have innate tendencies, and we are shaped by the world around us. *And* with hard work and determination, we have the power to modify even our most inherent propensities.

There are many ways to assess personality (which will

help you determine how curious you currently are), but I think the simplest and most straightforward is the Big Five personality inventory.[11] This assessment measures personality across five domains—openness to experience, conscientiousness, extroversion, agreeableness, and neuroticism. You can take the assessment online to see where you fall.

Openness to experience and conscientiousness are most closely related to curiosity. People who score high on openness tend to have a sense of adventure. They are more imaginative and curious, and they are open to a variety of experiences, especially intense experiences. Conversely, people who score low in openness tend to be more close-minded and dogmatic in their beliefs.

Individuals who score high on conscientiousness tend to be very disciplined and in control of their impulses. They maintain a sense of focus and determination when it comes to striving for achievement. Conversely, people who score low on conscientiousness tend to be more flexible, more spontaneous, and go with the flow—these are our curious folks. People who score high on openness and low on conscientiousness tend to be outside-the-box thinkers. They don't let anxiety get in the way of stepping outside of their comfort zones and don't avoid new situations due to fear of the unknown. They don't view setbacks as failures but as learning opportunities. Many of us exist somewhere in the middle. Maybe we are curious about some things but not others, but we can all work to expand and open our minds and experience the vast benefits of doing so regardless of where we score.

I could tell that given their personalities, both Richard and Naomi viewed the San Diego incident as a failure in their marriage. I wanted to help them shift their perspective to see this as a learning opportunity instead. What could they discover both separately and mutually that would help them grow from this experience? I decided to start by helping Richard think about his sexual value system. I've learned over the years that most people don't give much thought to their sexual values and certainly don't reevaluate them over time. We began with the following exercise.

Determining Your Sexual Values

What are sexual values?

Sexual values are comprised of your attitudes, beliefs, and feelings about what's right for you sexually.

Why are sexual values important?

Your values determine when you have sex, with whom you have sex, how you have sex, and under what conditions you have sex. Being clear about your sexual value system makes it easier to relax and enjoy the sex you're having. This clarity also makes it easier to select a partner with whom you can share long-term compatibility.

Answer the following questions to help you determine your sexual values.

1. How do you see the relationship between love and sex?
2. What safer-sex practices are important to you?
3. How important of a role do you want sex to play in your relationship?
4. What types of sexual activities do/don't you want to engage in?
5. How do you expect to be treated before/during/after sex?
6. What are your expectations about giving/receiving pleasure?
7. How comfortable are you with exploring sexual novelty?

8. What do you need to feel sexually satisfied?
9. Have you reevaluated your values now that you are older?
10. Have you talked to people who have different values from yours to fully understand different points of view?

I sat with Richard as he completed this exercise, and then we discussed his responses.

"I have never thought about some of these," he said. "I need some help understanding my feelings about love and sex and novelty. I'm still mixed up about how I feel regarding this whole thing in San Diego and how I felt with Naomi when I came home."

This is why I schedule individual sessions. I sensed that what Richard was about to say was something he'd never admit in front of his wife. He took a deep breath. "A part of me doesn't completely regret kissing my former colleague. I mean, obviously, I feel enormous guilt. I broke a vow to Naomi. I'm the kind of guy who follows through on my commitments, so this doesn't align with the principles that guide my life. But it was also exhilarating. As I mentioned, I didn't date much before settling down with Naomi. I was totally focused on academics, and plus, I was so young. I can't say that I've explored my sexuality apart from my experiences with Naomi since I've matured. The twenty-five-year-old version of myself never would have kissed an old fling in the elevator. I'm confident now in a way I wasn't back then."

I nodded compassionately, staying quiet so that he would elaborate.

"And you know what's even more confusing?" he started. "When I got home from the conference, Naomi and I made love in a way that felt more passionate than it had in years. I can't make sense of how I felt so connected to her despite the guilt that was there below the surface. I can't unfeel what I felt, and I'd be lying if I said I didn't want to feel it again."

I explained to Richard that the increased passion was likely due to a surge of adrenaline left over from the elevator kiss. We get plenty of adrenaline in the honeymoon phase, and it can certainly be cultivated later in a relationship, but not without a little bit of elbow grease. As we'll see, sexual novelty is one of the best ways to get a dose.

I decided to talk to both Richard and Naomi more about what they might be craving in the way of excitement and variety. I knew he didn't want to rely on lying to Naomi to get his fix. We'd need to find a way for them to identify what excited them and then figure out how to incorporate it into their relationship in a way that aligned with their shared value system.

At this point, you may have begun to consider what socially ascribed beliefs and values you may have unwittingly internalized and begun the process of discerning what fits versus what doesn't. You can begin to think about what you can do to add value, excitement, and interest to your life and talk to your partner about how to create space for that. Think about which parts of your personality—your sense of self—you've neglected, and imagine ways to get to know yourself again. You can begin the process individually, but it's also fun to do with a partner alongside you.

CREATING CURIOSITY IN YOUR RELATIONSHIP

Curiosity is key in keeping long-term relationships exciting. Studies find that curious people bond more easily to new friends than less curious folks because they actively cultivate intimacy in relationships.[12] These studies give us strong evidence that curiosity is an important quality, if not skill, in maintaining intimacy and closeness in relationships.

Relationship expert John Gottman strongly emphasizes the importance of maintaining curiosity in relationships.[13] He attests that maintaining a deep understanding of each other's worlds, or knowing your partner's *love maps*, is essential to maintaining a strong relationship. As my colleague Dr. Sara Nasserzadeh said, "We can't afford to just be curious; we have to be genuinely interested."[14] Maintaining a sense of curiosity within a relationship is vital. Relationships are dynamic over time. As they evolve, new meanings are created, stories are written, and futures are imagined. It is important that couples continuously get to know each other as their relationship progresses.

In my client sessions, I often apply what author Dr. Carol Dweck says in her book *Mindset* to relationships.[15] People who have a *fixed mindset* feel they have to prove themselves over and over again. They subscribe to the idea that intelligence is capped and personality is fixed. Alternatively, people who have a *growth* mindset believe that anything can be cultivated through effort, specific strategies, and support from others. How does mindset fit into romantic relationships? People with growth mindsets know that relationships take work, whereas people with fixed mindsets believe that if there is a major problem, the relationship must be doomed. They are also more likely to think that they should agree on just about everything with their partner because handling perpetual differences is intolerable for them. People with a fixed mindset are quick to assign blame when a conflict arises and attribute conflict to character flaws within their partner. People with a growth mindset, however, can more easily externalize the problem and address it head-on jointly with their partner.

Similarly, marriage researcher and author Dr. Eli Finkel distinguishes between happiness-based marriages and meaning-based marriages.[16] People who subscribe to a happiness-based model think marriage should be easy. Naomi and Richard fell into this camp. They admittedly created a life that was simple, predictable, and well . . . boring. People in the happiness-based model overemphasize pleasure and self-esteem and are more likely to jump ship when the going gets tough.

On the other hand, people who subscribe to the meaning-based model of marriage know that a healthy marriage takes work. They view the marriage as a springboard from which they can fully express who they are and discover that marital and personal fulfillment are totally compatible in the long run. I explained this to Naomi in the beginning of our individual session.

"Naomi, Richard mentioned that you used to paint and play the piano and that you were in law school at one point. While I totally understand putting those things on the back burner to focus on your family, I would also like to hear what makes you feel personally fulfilled apart from your role as a mother and wife."

Naomi looked at me, sadness in her eyes. "Nothing makes me feel more fulfilled than taking care of my family."

"I get it," I assured her.

She softened and then went on, "But yeah, I can't say I have much outside of that. If you were to ask me what my goals and ambitions are right now, I couldn't tell you. I know I don't want to go back to work. I could definitely carve out more time to paint."

"I think that would be a great start," I told her. "I'd like to ask you more specifically about your sexual interests. You said before that you're sexually available to Richard, but that word—*available*—feels passive to me. I'd like to see if understanding your personal sexuality would open the door to a clearer sense of self and even be an opportunity for personal fulfillment. What gets you excited? When does sex feel most passionate? What kinds of fantasies do you have?"

People always ask me why I chose to focus on sex therapy. There are many reasons, but one is that I always felt that you can learn so much about a person's psyche by asking questions about their sexuality. I was excited to see what unraveled with Naomi.

She took a deep breath. "Unlike Richard, I had plenty of experience before we started dating. I had several boyfriends and a few casual hookups thrown in for good measure." She winked. "I knew Richard had less experience, but it never bothered me. He's very attentive and responsive to the feedback I give him. I had some good boyfriends—some great lovers—but none of them were 'husband material.' Richard is a wonderful man, and like I said, I feel sexually satisfied with him. Do I sometimes long for a little more spice and excitement? Yeah, sure. But I wouldn't trade my life now for it. That's why this thing with Richard is so shocking. He risked everything—and for what?"

If I've heard it once, I've heard it a million times—the quintessential sex/love paradox—that *hot* sex—not "good enough" sex—but *hot* sex and lifelong companionship cannot fall hand in hand. I'm not willing to accept that, and I don't want my clients to feel like they need to either. I am a firm believer that with a growth mindset, the right tools, and plenty of trust, couples can cultivate the sex they want.

"Naomi," I said. "Does Richard know that in an ideal situation, you'd want a bit more out of your sex life?"

She slowly shook her head. "I don't want to hurt him," she said. "And I can't imagine he'd want to step too far outside the box. At least that's what I would have said a couple of months ago. Given what happened, now I'm not so sure."

While Naomi's actions had been considerate—she wanted to protect Richard's feelings—they had also caused her to unknowingly take part in her own dull sex life. Given what I'd learned about Richard—that a part of him didn't totally regret the kiss—I wondered if we were starting to unravel something below the surface of either of their consciousness—something that might enliven them both and create a more passionate sex life.

Like it or not, there are things you don't know about your partner. Again, this is why I like to meet individually with each person in a couple. Trust me when I say that everyone holds private thoughts and feelings. You can do one of two things with this awareness. You can feel intimidated and threatened, *or* you can feel excited by the fact that there is something about your partner you have yet to discover. I would go so far as to say that getting too comfortable is riskier than acknowledging the fact that there are hidden elements to everyone. As Esther Perel writes in *Mating in Captivity*, "Neutralizing each other's complexity affords us a kind of manageable otherness."[17] Diluting our partners sometimes makes them easier to manage (at least in the short term—look what happened to Richard and Naomi), but doesn't it also make them less exciting? And then, when our partners do something that is outside the norm, we feel thrown off and destabilized because it deviates from the way we see them. What would happen if instead of immediately protesting that they re-conform to the manageable otherness we've reduced them down to, we become curious about our instinctive reaction?

For many of us, it's automatic to approach an interaction with a fixed mindset. We may not even realize we are doing it. We often approach conflict or conversation with an agenda, closing our minds to what the other person might be thinking or feeling. In fact, most of us formulate a rebuttal before our partners have even finished their sentence. Creating space for our partners to fully express themselves helps get us out of our own narrow *perception* of the issue and opens us up to creating a shared *perspective*. This shift—from perception to perspective—helps us to more effectively problem solve. Try the following exercise to see the benefits of this shift.

From Old Perceptions to New Perspectives

Perception and perspective are similar but different. Your *perception* is unique to you. It is shaped by your experiences, emotions, beliefs, and values. Your perception shapes your interpretation of an issue. *Perspective* can be thought of as viewing the world through multiple perceptions, as if you are looking at an issue from the third person point of view. Couples can create a shared perspective by thoughtfully understanding each other's unique perceptions.

Couples often get locked into "my point of view" versus "their point of view" when dealing with conflict. Creating a shared perspective gives couples the opportunity to externalize the problem into one that can be tackled together as a team. This can only be accomplished with genuine curiosity and willingness to grow.

Repeating what your partner says is an essential component of this exercise. We often start formulating our rebuttal before our partner has finished their thought which creates a lot of misinterpretation. Parroting may feel silly, but trust me!

You Try It:

Sit face-to-face with your partner and make sure to remove any distractions.

Partner A: I would like to talk about (state the topic/conflict—keep it succinct).

Partner B: I hear you saying that you'd like to talk about (repeat the stated topic).

Partner A: About this issue, I think (share your thoughts) because (state a reason—related or from your past) and I feel (state your feeling).

Partner B: I hear you saying that you think (repeat Partner A's thought) because (repeat their reason) and you feel (repeat their feeling). Did I get that right?

Partner A: (This is your opportunity to correct anything Partner B missed or got wrong.)

Partner B: As it relates to (the topic), I think (share your thoughts) because (state a reason—related or from your past) and I feel (state your feeling).

Partner A: I hear you saying that you think (repeat Partner B's thought) because (repeat their reason) and you feel (repeat their feeling). Did I get that right?

Having heard and understood each other's perceptions, see if you can find common ground to create a joint perspective and plan to address the conflict. Is it easier to come up with a solution or at least a mutual, respectful understanding despite the difference?

By this point, I had encouraged Naomi and Richard to open up to each other about their desire to add some excitement and vitality back into their relationship. I walked them through the above exercise, and it went something like this.

Naomi: I'd like to talk about the San Diego incident.

Richard: Okay—you'd like to talk about the San Diego incident.

Naomi: I always thought of myself as the wilder one. I feel shocked because this is so unexpected but also intrigued as to what motivated you.

Richard: I hear you saying that you thought of yourself as the wilder one, which leaves you feeling shocked but also a little intrigued because this is so out of character for me. You want to understand my motivations. Did I get that right?

Naomi: Yes. Now I'd like to hear your perception.

Richard: I'm just as shocked as you are, but in that moment, I felt so overwhelmed by curiosity about this person and about the side of myself that was emerging, that it clouded my judgment. My thoughts at the time went out the window. When I think about it today, I think it did have something to do with rebelling against the expectations I and others have set for myself. That's the best reason I can come up with.

Naomi: I hear you saying that you were surprised as well but overtaken by curiosity about her and this latent side of yourself. You think the reason is it gave you an escape from some of the self-imposed confines of your life. Did I get that right?

Richard: Yes.

I stepped in. "Having heard each other's perceptions on what happened in San Diego, can you identify any commonalities that might help you create a new shared perspective?"

Richard shifted in his seat and then cleared his throat. "I didn't realize she used to be wilder. I'd like to learn more about that side of her because I think it's a side that's beginning to surface in myself. Maybe we have more in common than I realized."

In creating space to hear each other's perceptions on the thoughts and feelings related to the San Diego incident, Richard and Naomi were gradually able to create a new perspective—that they needed to shake things up in their relationship.

It's important to take steps to periodically push the relationship outside its everyday bounds. This helps break the cycle of monotony and gives you the opportunity to grow as individuals and as a couple. There are, of course, many ways to do this. It depends how hard you want to push. Going on a trip with nothing more than a rental car reservation, making a point to try a new restaurant once a month, or stepping outside your comfort zone to try a new class are all simple, wonderful ways to keep your relationship exciting.

For a lot of couples, shaking things up outside the bedroom is enough to create a sense of excitement inside the bedroom. I thought this would be a good place for Richard and Naomi to start. Rather than returning to the same beach rental they had every August for the past eight years, they decided to book a trip to the mountains. Naomi, who'd always painted, dropped her volunteer responsibilities at the kids' school for the semester and signed up for a ceramics class at the local art school instead. These new experiences were enough to gradually reawaken them to sides of themselves and each other that they'd been missing. Not only did they feel closer as a couple, the sex was beginning to feel more passionate too. Consider what you might try with your partner and then complete the following exercise.

Creating New Shared Experiences

Finding ways to be open to new experiences comes in many forms. If you've always been the kind of person to cozy up in a nice hotel while on vacation, try going on a camping or RV trip with your partner instead. If you typically prefer to dine at one of three favorite restaurants, push yourself to try a new spot at least once a month. If you are season ticket holders to your local sports team, try going to a play or concert once in a while. Sign up for a class you can do together like dance, cooking, or painting. Register for a lecture at your local university.

Try something new, and then answer these questions.

1. What did you think/feel before?
2. What did you think/feel during the activity?
3. What did you think/feel after the activity?
4. What did you learn about yourself?
5. What effect did this have on your relationship?

Trying new things with a long-term romantic partner can reignite feelings of passion. Psychologist Amy Muise researches this through self-expansion theory.[18] Through a series of studies, she and her colleagues found that people who tried something new like shucking an oyster for the first time or trying ballroom dance lessons were thirty-six times more likely to have sex with their partner that day— not twice as likely, a whopping thirty-six times more likely! The boost in desire that people experienced had broader implications, including greater relationship and sexual satisfaction. Perhaps most exciting, they found that these positive results were sustained over time.

If you recall from my own research project, the more curious we are as individuals, the more sexually satisfied we tend to be.[19] What this means is that the vitality and excitement we feel from learning new things translates synergistically into our sex lives. This is something that Kleinplatz identified in her research as well. She writes that among her research participants, "the emphasis was not on new sexual acts or props but on creating a context for revealing one another anew and in even deeper ways." She found that there is a balance that is "required between discovery and trust, which in turn creates an atmosphere rich with 'anticipated surprise.'"[20]

As we'll see more clearly in the next section, maintaining a sense of curiosity—about yourself, your partner, and the world around you—fosters energy and newness into your sex life without necessarily trying anything new. That's what's so fun about this. It's more about being connected with a new or forgotten side of yourself. It's that intangible, energetic shift that can create such an exciting intensity, even in long-term relationships.

CULTIVATING CURIOSITY IN EROTICISM

An entire book could be written about sexual curiosity, but in an effort to narrow it down to the most important elements, I've decided to focus on three paths. First, I'll elaborate on the concept of how sex can be an opportunity to discover new sides of yourself and your partner. Next, we'll explore how to tap into the curious, erotic mind by learning about the nature of sexual fantasies. And finally, we'll dive into the psychology of sexual novelty and learn how to apply the science of flow to take sexual exploration to new heights.

Most of us don't ask questions about who we are as sexual beings. You probably didn't grow up with parents who asked you questions like those I posed in the Determining Your Sexual Values exercise. I always tell people that you cannot separate your individuality from your sexuality. Everything that makes you who you are is going to come through as elements of your sexuality. But for a lot of people, sex becomes a mere physical act as opposed to a form of individual, relational, and emotional expression, which is part of the reason so many people feel dissatisfied with it.

There has been a long-standing belief that excitement, novelty, and spontaneity stand apart from familiarity, safety, and security. This couldn't be further from the truth. Creativity lives in the space between that which is familiar and that which is new. The familiarity of a long-term partner and the newness of experiences outside (or inside) the bedroom can be the two most potent ingredients for sexual vitality. This is the power of curiosity. It does not mean that you have to experiment with new techniques, toys, or positions (although this can be great fun too!). Instead, it means that you can explore sex as a way to celebrate, comfort, heal, cherish, and so much more.

Studies show that couples who maintain high levels of sexual satisfaction over the course of long-term relationships find that some of the best sex comes after going through meaningful transitions in life together as a couple.[21] Having a baby is without a doubt one of life's biggest transitions. A lot of us think having a new baby kills eroticism (and for a lot of couples, it temporarily does),[22] but then I spoke to Cynthia and Jason, a couple who participated in my research study. Cynthia had not been cleared for intercourse, but she and her husband found other ways of staying sexually connected. She said that one of the best sexual experiences they shared was a passionate, very handsy make-out session in the shower one night after the baby had fallen asleep. She described herself melting into the kiss as they devoured each other under the hot water. She said that she felt an intensity and love for her husband, a feeling of wonder about having created a human together. I always thought this was such a beautiful example of how going through something meaningful can deepen intimacy that translates directly into sexual passion.

I've also spoken to couples who go through trying times and turn to sex as a way to comfort each other. Doing so can help us reconnect with eros, which is our love and life force (the opposite of Thanatos, which in Greek mythology is the personification of death). Miranda, another one of my research participants, described how she found comfort in her wife after the premature death of her twin sister. "I look back now, and I can't imagine how I was in the mood that week. But one rainy afternoon, we ended up making love. She held me for hours. There was something about it that acted as a salve for my broken heart."

I want to encourage you to think about how attaching meaning to sex can be a gateway to experiencing a heightened state of passion and connection. Sex is so much more than a juxtaposition of body parts. It is a bouquet of the emotional, psychological, relational, and spiritual elements of yourself and your partner. Consider how you can use your curious mind to make sex more passionate. Think about it this way. How do you feel when you see your partner in different roles—ready to tackle the boardroom at work, dressed up for a night out, cuddling with your child in the soft morning light, goofing off with old friends, or relaxing with family? We have so many sides of our personality that come out depending on our environment and the people that surround us. So why do so many people feel hesitant to express different sides of themselves during sex? I maintain that the bedroom is the optimal place to explore different sides of our personality, especially sides that no one else sees. When you have a partner who makes you feel safe (more on that in chapter 4), you have all you need to explore each other—your dominant side, your playful side, your tender side, or your submissive side. Sex gives you the opportunity to celebrate, to cherish, to romance, to connect, to explore, to nurture, to comfort, and so much more. And it all starts by leaning into curiosity. Explore the meaning of your sexual interaction with the following exercise.

Creating Novelty Through Meaning

We have the power to use the emotional climate of our lives to create a sense of meaning in our everyday sexual experiences. The variations of this meaning, emotion, and energy can add to the "sense" of novelty in our sex lives without actually trying anything new. In safe, loving relationships, sexual connection can be an opportunity to heal, celebrate, connect, comfort, and more.

You Try It:

Reflect on the current emotional climate of your relationship. You can even think more broadly. What are you feeling at work? What is happening with your extended family? What is happening nationally or globally?

Now think about what you need right now. Do you need compassion or comfort? Is there something you want to celebrate? Is something going on from which you need an escape? Have you gone through something painful and you need healing energy?

Talk to your partner about what you're experiencing. Discuss ways you can use your sexual connection to provide what you need. Maybe you want a long, slow, nurturing massage before progressing further. Perhaps you need the adrenaline rush of a quickie in a place you could get caught. Perhaps you need to enact a spanking scenario to relieve pent-up energy. Come up with ways that you can use sex to give you what you need emotionally or as an opportunity to express an emotion you may be experiencing.

When we keep open and curious minds, sex can help us discover hidden parts of our psyches, explore our emotional sides, and even be a way to heal old traumas. Dustin, an executive at a Fortune 500 company, enjoyed visiting a dominatrix from time to time. Being told what to do provided a respite from being the boss. Maxine, who was homeschooled in a small town in Arkansas, enjoyed role-playing a naughty high school football cheerleader since she'd never had this experience in real life. Jessica and Ewan described a passionate, celebratory romp in the sheets when she was accepted to the business program of her dreams. Violet sheepishly admitted to makeup sex being her favorite. She described the way her longtime boyfriend seemed to hungrily ravish her body as if it were the first time. Reconnecting not just physically but also emotionally after an argument felt both new and familiar.

Naomi and Richard were no different. Naomi confessed how much passion she felt the first time she and Richard had sex after he confessed what he'd done. She didn't understand how her desire could be amplified in the wake of the relationship betrayal. I explained that a phenomenon known as *mate guarding* was probably at play.[23] This happens both in the animal kingdom and among humans when sexual or reproductive access to a mate feels threatened.

"Whatever you want to call it," she said skeptically, "I liked the rush. I haven't felt that in a while. Of course, I'd like to find other ways of getting it. I don't want to go through this again."

As we'll see, there are plenty of exciting (and ethical) ways to get the rush. A simple way, which you can do all on your own, is to tap into the world of sexual fantasy.

Think your fantasies are unusual? Think again. One of the largest studies on sexual fantasies surveyed 4,175 American adults of all income brackets, races, religions, political affiliations, and sexual and gender identities who were involved in an array of relationship styles and found that 97 percent of them reported having sexual fantasies.[24] The study's author, Dr. Justin Lehmiller, found that most sexual fantasies fall into seven broad categories. The top three are multiple partners, BDSM, and sexual novelty and adventure. The remaining four categories are taboo/forbidden sex, nonmonogamy, passion and romance, and flexibility/gender-bending. Suffice it to say that the majority of people's fantasies would make your mother blush (except for the fact that, chances are, she's having steamy fantasies herself!).

When my clients open up to me about their sexual fantasies, they often do so with shame and embarrassment. Many are mortified to even admit that they have a fantasy, let alone tell me exactly what it is. As a species, we are uniquely able to visualize different narratives for ourselves and play out imagined scenes in our minds. If we do this in other areas of our lives, why shouldn't we do it sexually? And furthermore, why feel bad about it?

Fantasies are wonderful because they are always free, they are always accessible, and they're completely safe.[25] There's no reason why you shouldn't tap into your fantasy world. Having an active fantasy life can keep the proverbial wheel greased. The largest sex organ sits between your ears, not your legs, and fantasy is a great way to keep your brain in gear.

At the end of the day, it's up to you whether you share

your fantasies with your partner or keep them to yourself. Both can lead to enhanced pleasure with your partner.

Too many people feel threatened or intimidated when they learn their partner has fantasies beyond what the two of them explore. Having a fantasy world does not mean that you don't love your partner. It doesn't mean that you're unhappy with your sex life, and it doesn't necessarily mean that you want something or someone else in real life. As I said before, our ability to conjure and explore mental images is a uniquely human quality. When we admonish ourselves for having a specific fantasy, misconstrue it as cheating on our partners, or see it as a sign that we're not into our partners, what we're effectively doing is cutting off a little bit of our humanness. As I always say, just because you already ordered doesn't mean you can't look at the menu. How many times have you imagined traveling to places you'll probably never go? Have you ever thought about how it would feel to climb Mount Everest knowing full well you never will? Why? Because allowing ourselves to think about the impossible, improbable, unlikely, and extraordinary is fun. Having a rich fantasy life on your own can cultivate a sexual energy, excitement, and zest that spills over into partnered sex. Fantasy is a wonderful gateway to sexual curiosity and exploration. Richard and Naomi were no exception. She'd admitted to this whole experience triggering memories about her own past sexual experiences, and he said that despite his best efforts to forget the San Diego kiss, he couldn't stop thinking about it. I began to wonder if fantasy alone would be enough for them or if they might chart new territory as a couple.

By this point, things had stabilized between Richard and

Naomi. They had worked hard to reestablish trust. They broke the monotony of their relationship by trying new things and felt an immediate positive effect on their sex life. They returned to therapy eager to tell me how much more connected they felt both emotionally and sexually, but they also wanted help processing a recent conversation they'd had.

"Tell me what's going on," I prompted.

"Well," said Naomi. "Richard and I admitted to each other that we both have some lingering excitement, or curiosity even, about his kiss in San Diego. I'm struggling to make sense of it because on the one hand, I feel extremely jealous, but on the other hand, I feel a little turned on."

Richard picked up where she left off. "I'm struggling too because while I feel completely recommitted to Naomi, the incident revealed an itch I didn't know I had. When Naomi told me she still felt a little turned on about it, I confessed that I did too. We're not sure what to do with these feelings."

"I have to applaud you for being curious about these feelings," I told them. "Most people wouldn't acknowledge them at all or would, at best, just stuff them back down where they came from. You know by now that it's normal to have sexual fantasies that involve other people, and for plenty of folks, exploring them internally or across the pillow from their partner is enough to keep things exciting. But these days, it's becoming more common for couples to explore their sexuality in actuality. Is this something you want to talk about?"

They looked at each other with hesitation. Whether or not they'd said so out loud, I could tell they both anticipated that this was where the conversation might turn. I knew it would be best to start with an explanation about the psychology of novelty. I wanted to offer tips to help them take baby steps so they wouldn't feel overwhelmed or fall victim to the emotional risk that is always present when couples decide to push the relationship to new bounds.

There are countless books about how to spice things up, and while the benefits of curiosity expand far beyond trying new things in the bedroom, it's worth discussing this fun component of sexual exploration. We have plenty of evidence[26] to support the idea that sexual novelty is a key in long-term sexual satisfaction, and you can't explore new things without first being mutually curious about what you might try. When I asked my research participants what made the run-of-the-mill sexual encounter different from an optimal one, they said it was when they hit that perfect mix of emotional security and spontaneity. It's hard to feel safe enough to explore new things if you don't feel emotionally secure in your relationship. Now that Richard and Naomi had reestablished trust and reconnected as a couple, they could begin to explore new dimensions of their relationship. They were committed to finding a way to experience the erotic rush again. They wanted sex that made them forget the world around them. What they wanted . . . was to experience flow.

A flow state, which is what so many people want to experience during sex, lies between the space of familiarity and novelty. One of Mihaly Csikszentmihalyi's most important components of flow is the challenge/skills balance. As you can see in the image on the next page, there is a sweet spot when the challenge of what you're doing is just slightly above your skill set. It's nestled in this sweet spot that we experience the blissful state of flow. If the challenge is too weak, you'll feel bored. If it's too high, you'll feel anxious. Presence, focus, and pleasure show up when the challenge is just a hair outside the norm.

In helping other clients achieve a flow state in sex, I'd seen couples move too fast or too slow through sexual exploration, and I wanted to make sure Naomi and Richard didn't make the same mistakes. My clients Sarah and Eloise, for instance, came to see me after several failed attempts at spicing things up. In their first attempt, they had decided to experiment with bondage. Sarah blindfolded Eloise and tied her to the bed, but Eloise, noticing an unpleasant sensation of anxiety building, blurted out the safe word just as Sarah was attaching the nipple clamps. Unfortunately, the buildup of tension had the opposite effect. Eloise, excited, but also nervous about what she couldn't see, had a hard time loosening up and found it impossible to relax enough for arousal to build. Deciding to take things slower the next time, they tried again a few weeks later. Eloise surprised Sarah with a new sex toy she'd found online. Sarah appreciated the thought, but it was very similar to something she'd tried before. They ended up having a good time, but it didn't do much to elevate their sexual connection.

Where did Sarah and Eloise go wrong? Their first attempt was too far outside of Eloise's comfort level (or skill set), which ended up creating too much anxiety for her. Their next attempt was too far below Sarah's experience, which is why the sexual interaction felt lackluster. I helped them identify some behaviors that were just the right balance, which eventually resulted in the rush of adrenaline they were both longing for.

Where exactly is that sweet spot, and how do you go about identifying it? Research shows that the challenge only needs to be about 4 percent greater than your skills.[27] That's it. Any more than that, and a stretch is likely to turn into a snap. You'll know you're ready to stretch when you feel optimistic and excited by the challenge as opposed to nervous or overwhelmed.

I knew that giving Richard and Naomi some information about opening up would be a good first step. Information is power, and the more they knew, the less anxious they'd feel. I started by normalizing their feelings. I told them that a lot of people experience a boost in sexual desire when a new partner is introduced. This is known as the *Coolidge effect*. People can then choose whether to channel the desire to the new partner *or* intentionally transfer the new-relationship energy to sex with their primary partner, which intensifies passion.

I explained that there are many misconceptions about consensual nonmonogamy. First, not all couples choose to practice full-on polyamory. Some play with being *monogamish*, a term that means couples are monogamous the majority of the time, but give each other, for example, permission to flirt or hook up with others while traveling for work. Another misconception, according to research by psychologist Dr. Amy Moors, is that consensual nonmonogamy is only practiced by a "certain kind" of person. In fact, studies have found no differences across people across geographical location, income, age, political affiliation, race/ethnicity, or education level.[28] The idea among people who practice consensual nonmonogamy, I explained, is that romantic love and sexual desire are not seen as commodities that can run out. Just like we can love more than one friend or child, people in consensually nonmonogamous relationships feel they can connect romantically and/or sexually with more than one person.

It doesn't come without its own drawbacks, of course. I explained that jealousy and even heartbreak are real emotions that people deal with even if they've consented to opening up. I reminded them that it takes a couple in a strong, healthy relationship to minimize risk, and whether or not it works largely depends on whether you have the right personality to tolerate it. Finally, it shouldn't be considered a solution for an otherwise failing relationship. I reminded them we could explore other ways of introducing novelty. I could give them resources on BDSM, tantra, and role-play, but they decided to stick with exploring the thoughts and feelings they were currently having.

Naomi and Richard were intrigued but still felt apprehensive about the idea. It reminded me of something that flow researcher Steven Kotler wrote about the relationship between anxiety and curiosity. He says,

> Neurobiologically, anxiety and curiosity are opposite sides of the same coin. They're both a response to uncertainty . . . and this means we can use curiosity to fight anxiety. [Curiosity helps us] recognize anxiety as it's beginning to arise, before it becomes a thought and demands more energy. This is why curiosity and creativity are clutch. They're skill sets that help us manage anxiety in the present, while unlocking possibility in the future.[29]

There are a few things to keep in mind when you're reaching for your 4 percent. Researchers have determined that confidence, optimism, mindset (which we've already talked about), actual skills, tolerance for anxiety, ability to delay gratification, and societal values all play a role.[30] Confidence, optimism, and mindset all influence how easy the challenge *feels*. As Kotler described in the passage above, anxiety and curiosity can go hand in hand. Your ability to stretch to 4 percent may be affected by the degree to which you can tolerate the discomfort required to grow. We'll talk about this more in the next chapter. If unease makes you squeamish, you're unlikely to strike flow. Finally, societal values, as we've learned, can impede how comfortable we are with sexual curiosity. If you grew up with the message that sexual experimentation was wrong, chances are you'll stay safe (but bored). The best course of action is to go slowly. There is no shame in starting off with just 1 or 2 percent as you ease into your flow zone.

I advise couples to talk through ideas before mutually agreeing on something that strikes the right balance of challenge and skills. Having an open conversation goes a long way in reducing anxiety so that you can focus on the playful elements of curiosity. I usually give couples a comprehensive checklist of different things they might try. We discuss which items they would consider trying, which items they definitely want to try, and which they have no interest in trying. We process the feelings they have around each sex act to create as much overlap as possible between their preferences. Then I have them take baby steps as they begin to explore together. This approach gives them the best likelihood that novelty will have the intended effect. Check the appendix at the back of the book to see my complete "Identifying Sexual Likes and Dislikes" exercise.

I walked Richard and Naomi through a version of this exercise, one that focused on different things they might do that involved other people. After several sessions, they agreed to start by giving each other permission to flirt or go so far as sharing a drink with someone else. They weren't keen on the idea of crossing a physical or sexual boundary with other people. They decided to experiment with flirting and then assess whether they could effectively manage the feelings they had about it. This decision gave Richard the opportunity to put himself out there with women in a way he hadn't before, and it put Naomi back in touch with a side of herself she'd long forgotten. Richard, being the more cautious of the two, wanted to take things very slowly. They were committed to each other above all else and didn't want to do anything to compromise their relationship. Just getting to this point had deepened intimacy and renewed passion in a way they'd never experienced before. They wanted to ride the wave, not crash to the ocean floor.

If, like Naomi, you're the one in the relationship with more anxiety tolerance, you do what any good teammate would do. You remain patient, encouraging, and supportive until your partner approximates your level of readiness. If you're the one with less experience, you use the emotional security you have with your partner as a bolster as you push through the initial discomfort of growth before finding your 4 percent.

It is important to move slowly when trying new things. You need to give your brain time to process new information and implement it into new patterns. When this happens, you'll get little boosts of dopamine, which will help you feel more motivated, and eventually lead to the flow zone.

I caution people about going for something totally out of their sexual norm without a conversation first. Make sure your partner feels comfortable with what you have in mind, and invite them to cocreate ideas with you. Two heads are better than one, and it's important that you're clear on each other's limits. If your partner suggests something and you notice an automatic *no* reaction, try to switch on that curious mind. Ask yourself what your automatic reaction is about. A lot of people hold negative preconceived notions about different sex acts, but, as with anything, you can't say for sure how you'll feel about something until you try it (sometimes not until you try it a couple of times).

Reassess and consider whether your *no* might actually

be a *maybe*. There may be some things that are a hard no for you, and that's okay, but I bet you'd be willing to try more than you initially think after hacking your curious mind. A 2017 study of nearly forty thousand heterosexual adults in long-term relationships found that sexual novelty was a key player among those with the highest levels of sexual satisfaction.[31] Again, if you are in an emotionally safe and loving relationship, you should feel secure enough to try something new here and there (more on this in the next chapter!). You don't have to end up loving everything. If there is something that ultimately you decide you don't like, at least it becomes a shared experience, which enhances intimacy. Maybe it's something that you have a good laugh about down the road.

Having a curious mind makes us healthier individuals, more interesting partners, and more optimal lovers. As we learned from Richard and Naomi, curiosity can awaken parts of ourselves we've lost and reinvigorate our relationship in ways we never imagined. While only you and your partner can determine how far you'll let curiosity guide you on your journey of exploration, my hope is that this chapter inspired you to tap into this vital part of yourself. Don't be afraid to challenge long-held assumptions and beliefs, which may be inhibiting your ability to reach your full potential as an individual and in your partnership. Reawakening your curious mind can be scary, but with the right tools, a supportive partner, and a determination to grow, I feel confident you'll agree with me that curiosity didn't kill the cat. It freed her.

3

THE POWER OF ADAPTABILITY

Turn and face the strange.
—"Changes" by David Bowie

When I was twenty-five, I planned a trip to Cuba with my father, who had not returned to his native country since fleeing in 1960, after the revolution. We no longer had relatives there, but we went to visit some good family friends. Like most Cubans today, they lived in a house that had been subdivided to accommodate several families. It had been bright pink in its prime, but like many of the buildings in Cuba, the color had faded, and it was crumbling bit by bit. Rosarito lived on the top floor. We climbed two flights of stairs, which seemed surprisingly easy for her given that she was nearly eighty years old and was puffing away on what was likely her fifth unfiltered cigarette of the day. We passed families who lived on the other levels, their doors open to let in what relief the June breeze could bring, and they kindly waved hello as we walked up.

She guided us inside, and I could instantly smell the intoxicating aroma of freshly brewed Cuban coffee. When we entered the living room, we noticed the furniture had been moved to the perimeter. The sun was shining down on us, causing us to turn our gazes upward. There was a gaping hole in the ceiling, about the size of a dining table. She followed our shocked expressions, rolling her eyes and shrugging. "Don't worry," she said, "this allows us to dance under the stars." She explained that the roof had caved in a few months prior, and they were still waiting for the government to come and do repairs. In the meantime, she was sleeping with her dear friend and neighbor one floor below.

We offered our sympathy, but she brushed it off. "Please," she said, "we are used to it. We were dealt a bad hand of cards. We chose to stay. We make the most of it. You can't let it get to you. We are happy anyway."

How is it, I often wondered, that in Cuba, under the restrictions of an oppressive dictatorship, people seemed to enjoy an internal freedom that I wasn't seeing here in the United States—a place that is literally touted as "the land of the free and the home of the brave"? I saw Cubans dancing in the streets and playing music along the Malecón. Meanwhile, it occurred to me that over the years, Americans had gone from fearlessly exploring new frontiers to impatiently waiting in the pharmacy line to refill their antidepressants.

It was on this trip that my new therapeutic model started to form. I wanted to find a way to teach my clients to pursue joy despite the hardships they faced in life. I wanted to give them better tools to adapt to life's hurdles so they could get back to enjoying sex. My clients seemed to be so stressed out all the time. It was clear that their anxiety and worry were holding them back from enjoying one of life's greatest pleasures. I thought about what I had seen on this trip and returned to my office determined to apply some new techniques. It wasn't long before the perfect test couple came in.

Sydney and Shane were in their midthirties and came to see me for help reconnecting sexually. Shane worked as a commercial architect, and Sydney was a project manager at a large interior design firm. They met in college at an '80s-themed party. "It was the neon high heels for me," Shane said with a smile. Sydney rolled her eyes and elbowed him playfully in the ribs. It was a good sign they still had a lighthearted side to their relationship. I wondered where things had gone awry.

Sydney took a deep breath before sharing their story. I noticed her right foot start to tap nervously on the floor. "We're here because we rarely have sex anymore, and when we do, it is a disappointment for both of us." Shane's smile faded, and he shifted uncomfortably in his seat. Sydney continued, "I feel like it started because of me. I had a difficult pregnancy and birth, and while I don't want to blame the baby, I'd be remiss if I didn't tell you that life was a complete nightmare the first year. It's a total blur, and even though he's great now"—their son was now five years old and thriving at the local elementary school—"the damage was done. I was completely uninterested in sex for a long time. Sex hurt as I was recovering from my episiotomy, and emotionally, I wasn't into it. I guess I'm still not into it since having Devon."

I looked at Shane. His cue to share. "Yeah. To say the first year was rough is an understatement. We were in total survival mode. I don't think either of us was interested in sex, but eventually, things calmed down, and we tried. And failed. And tried. And failed."

"What do you mean—you failed?" I asked.

Shane continued, "It had been so long since we'd made

love, I came within a minute the first time. It obviously wasn't great for Sydney, which she made clear. That's why she blames herself. She thinks her negative reaction and general disinterest in sex created a 'complex' for me. I can't say it helped, but I'm sure there is more to it than that. We didn't try again for a while. When we did, I was so nervous, I couldn't get it up. I don't think that's ever happened to me. Sydney was cool about it the next time, but now we are stuck in a vicious cycle. I've developed performance anxiety, and neither of us is interested anymore. The pills aren't even helping."

Shane had spoken with his family physician. His hormones were normal, so his doctor prescribed a PDE5 inhibitor. It helped a little, but his erections still weren't as good as they had been prior. And when he did get one, he was so afraid of losing it that he came quickly, which frustrated them both.

Sydney jumped in. "It wasn't always like this. Sex used to make us feel connected. We had several wonderful years together before having Devon. We made love all over the place. It was spontaneous and fun. Now it feels completely robotic. I'm turned off. He's turned off. That version of us feels so far gone, I can't imagine getting it back. At this point, I'd be happy with five-out-of-ten sex."

I nodded in understanding and smiled at them sympathetically. I knew how to help Shane recover his erections and regain some ejaculatory control, but would that suffice? She may have said she would be satisfied with five-out-of-ten sex, but I had a feeling that wouldn't be enough in the long run, especially if they'd enjoyed more passionate sex in the years before kids. Furthermore, I knew that while most people think orgasms and erections are the barometers for good sex, the research says otherwise. I imagined that the longing Shane felt to regain his erection paled in comparison to the longing he had to reconnect erotically with his wife the way they once had. I asked more about their life. I wanted to understand how parenthood had affected them on a broader scale.

It came as no surprise that their sex life wasn't the only thing that had suffered. Shane felt enormous self-induced pressure to provide for his family. He was riddled with guilt about not earning enough for Sydney to quit work. He was convinced she'd be less wound up if she had more time for herself. She, however, insisted she didn't want to quit. She loved her job. It gave her a sense of identity apart from her role as a wife and mother. They found themselves bickering constantly about him not "getting her," but she admitted she struggled to understand herself now too. She was traumatized from that first year with the baby, and her lingering anxiety spilled over into other areas of her life. In an effort to keep everything under control, she'd become obsessive—about what their son ate, maintaining a sleep schedule, buying only Montessori-approved toys. Parenting books had replaced her favorite novels.

Shane wasn't off the hook. While he assumed his premature ejaculation was because they hadn't had sex in a while, I suspected there was something deeper going on. I wondered if his preoccupation with being the sole breadwinner had affected the way he saw himself as a man and if this affected his virility as a result. Sydney's anxiety was more obvious, but Shane had his own worries lurking below the surface. As I listened to the description of their life now versus before, it became clear that despite their best efforts, they had not adapted to parenthood as well as they had thought.

WHAT IS ADAPTABILITY?

Put simply, adaptability describes one's ability to adjust to new conditions or circumstances. It is about resilience in the face of adversity. This is one of my favorite secrets because it focuses on how to cultivate a relationship and sex life that stand the test of time. The honeymoon period of the relationship is easy. Everything is new, and two people are falling in love, and all is good in the world. Our love, we believe, can conquer all. But then, a decade in, with a crying kid and a stack of bills and dinner burning on the stove, our problems suddenly feel insurmountable. Rather than believing our love for each other can gracefully pole-vault us through life, we find ourselves blaming and resenting the very person we thought we cherished. We realize we lack the tools to effectively tackle our problems in ways that won't result in resenting our partners. Rather than working together, we notice a chasm gradually widen. Our partners become our adversaries. It's no wonder that so many people start to feel like sex is a chore as opposed to the thing they couldn't wait to do in the early days. If this sounds familiar, keep reading.

This chapter will show you how to work with your partner instead of against them. I'll explain how you can grow from adversity and how you can use new tools to maintain passion even when life tries to take you down. Good sex, after all, is one of the most wonderful escapes from trying times. It's also a space in which we can heal and discover life and love again.

Curiosity is a prerequisite for adaptability. Formulating new ideas and having a growth mindset is part of it, but adaptability is also about having the courage to implement change. You'd think our modern-day lifestyle would make it easy to adapt. But the paradox is that while we have more resources at our fingertips than ever before, we seem to have lost our problem-solving skills. We've begun to lose what was once a natural ability to adapt to the unplanned and make do with less. Uncertainty used to be a natural part of life, but now we have so many apps and tools designed to make the uncertain certain that we've lost sight of how to navigate the unknown.

The human species has adapted to survive in pretty much any environment. You will not see a polar bear surviving in the Sahara, nor will you see a camel surviving in the Arctic. Humans, however, have adapted to survive in just about every climate. Naturally, there are some individual differences, but as a species, humans have found a way. If this is the case, why can we be so resistant to change? Do we or don't we have a natural inclination toward adaptability? What makes one person more or less willing to lean into the unknown and adapt to change? And how does this all relate to sex?

A lot of people view their lives like a stack of cards, believing that if they don't do everything in their power to keep their lives in perfect order, everything will come crashing down. Think of Sydney, white-knuckling her way through motherhood in an attempt to keep everything under control, or Shane, who felt totally derailed by the loss of his erection and ejaculatory control. It doesn't help that we are bombarded with images of people who seem to "do life" with perfection and ease. Social media has created a complete illusion of the realities of most people's lives. The truth is, life gets messy. Things happen that we can't anticipate or never would have planned for. We are faced with unexpected tragedies, loss, illness, and betrayal. Our beliefs may change, our feelings evolve. It's how we handle these ups and downs that makes us resilient, give our lives meaning, and at the end of the day, brings intensity, depth, and passion into our sexual experiences. Shane and Sydney thought that they'd adapted well to parenthood. They'd read all the books, hadn't they? So why did they both feel so on edge all the time? Why had erotic connection become such a massive struggle? I suspected their underlying anxiety was at play. Anxiety and fear are two of the biggest blocks to adaptability. Let's explore why.

BARRIERS TO ADAPTABILITY

A certain level of anxiety is necessary. Fear and anxiety are completely natural and important feelings. In fact, all our emotions, whether they feel good or bad, comfortable or uncomfortable, serve a purpose. It is important, therefore, that we never ignore or dismiss our "negative" emotions. Anxiety is the body's natural response to stress. It signals to us that something is wrong or that danger might be present. Mild to moderate anxiety may cause us to experience a tightness in the chest, butterflies in the stomach, or shortness of breath. Our palms may break out into a sweat. The presence of anxiety in new situations or environments—public speaking, going on a first date, or going for a job interview, for example—keeps us on our toes. If we appear too relaxed in a job interview, HR may think we're not taking it seriously.

Zero anxiety on a first date makes it less likely we'll notice red flags. This is adaptive. A little bit of anxiety forces us to pay closer attention to all the information that surrounds us, something that is important when in a new environment or with a new person. Anxiety as we enter parenthood is no exception. A little bit of hypervigilance ensures survival of the species. I explained as much to Shane and Sydney, but also expressed some concern that at five years down the line, some of their particular anxieties—her worry about their son and his concern about his ability to provide for the family—seemed to have gotten the best of them and were affecting their ability to connect in the bedroom. Shane and Sydney, like most people, have a "picture" of how their life, their relationship, and their sex should look. When suddenly any of the three don't appear as they feel they should, they might find themselves stuck rather than up to the challenge of adapting.

Severe anxiety can be debilitating, paralyzing us and preventing us from moving forward and adapting. This is problematic because as a society, we are more anxious than we've ever been in history. When our bodies are flooded with overwhelming stress signals, we enter fight, flight, or freeze mode. This signal evolved as a survival mechanism to protect us from life-threatening situations. Imagine living thousands of years ago. You are out on the hunt, and a saber-toothed tiger crosses your path. You have two choices: get out of there (flight) or try to attack the tiger (fight). Assuming you are successful in either killing the tiger or getting away, you go back to your tribe and *relax* until it's time for the next hunt. Your tribe, by the way, is a group of people you've lived alongside every waking moment since you were born. It's not a new group of people you're forcing small talk with at a happy hour (cue social anxiety).

The problem today is that we overload ourselves with so much moderate stress on a daily basis that our brains send constant, sometimes chronic signals that danger might be imminent. The result is a constant uptick in anxiety. Think back to our discussion of multitasking in chapter 1. We overload our systems with so much information that we short-circuit. In other words, our brains and bodies haven't evolved to effectively cope with the way we live our lives. Add to that the pressure society puts on us to be everything and do it all—of course we're prone to snap!

We are seeing an overwhelming increase in health issues directly related to stress. Stress can lead to heart conditions, digestive issues, high blood pressure, weight gain, insomnia, and other health conditions. Stress also makes underlying issues, such as autoimmune conditions, worse.[1] And stress, we know for certain, gets in the way of the body's sexual response. Why would your body distract you with an erection in the presence of a saber-toothed tiger?

Too many of my clients are stressed out, overwhelmed, and unhappy despite having roofs over their heads and clean water to drink. (I'm not saying this from a place of judgment. I've dealt with bouts of anxiety myself.) Many of them come to therapy looking to me for a quick fix, a wave of a magic wand to solve their problems. So, what is actually happening here? Why does it seem so hard to embrace the unknown these days? Why do so many people seem at a complete loss for how to cope with relationship ups and downs? What about what Friedrich Nietzsche said: *What doesn't kill me makes me stronger?* These days, it seems to me that what doesn't kill us makes us weaker. Adversity, due to the anxiety and uncertainty it creates, seemed to be splintering my couples, not bringing them closer. Furthermore, I noticed an increasingly high percentage of clients say that chronic stress and anxiety were to blame for their lack of libido. This was frustrating for me as a sex therapist because I always viewed sex as an opportunity to escape the turmoil of our day-to-day.

Filmmaker Jason Silva posted a video sharing how sex gives him an escape from the anxiety present in his life. I love how poetically he shares his views, and his words echoed what I am trying to communicate here. He said,

> *I think in some sense, my desire for intimacy is coupled to my desire to heal from the alienation, separation, and hypervigilance that characterizes so much of the ruminating anxiousness . . . that has been my lived experience when I'm not in the zone. But when I'm safe, when I'm held, when I'm seen, when I'm vanishing, I enter a realm of a new kind of intimacy . . . I merge with whoever I'm with. I become what I behold. I lose all fear and all identity and all temporality, and instead enter the realm of Eden. I go into paradisical places where I'm psychologically skinny dipping and hopefully naked in flesh as well. I am finally in the realm of love. I am finally in the blue lagoon. I'm finally in a Mediterranean dream . . . We are kissing and we live to see another day at the edge of time, we are eternal beings, blazing into the sunset together, and the throngs of reverie and communion and blissfuck. This is what I mean by intimacy. This is what I am so hungry for.[2]*

Look at some of the phrases Silva uses—"I become what I behold," "in the zone," "loss of fear and temporality." He's talking about flow. He's talking about using sex as an opportunity to experience flow in a way that makes him forget the ever-present anxiety in the world around him. I wanted to help my clients see it in the same light.

Anxiety makes us worry incessantly about what has happened, what is happening now, or what might happen in the future. Fear of the unknown is a big source of anxiety for many folks. Constant, overwhelming worry can become debilitating, causing some people to grow a protective barrier around themselves, making emotional and physical intimacy a real challenge.

Shane, upon his first experience with "performance" anxiety, immediately withdrew. Sydney, paralyzed by her postpartum anxiety, could no longer surrender to the pleasures of sex or even tap into her own desire, for that matter. I explained to Shane that he had developed anticipatory anxiety. He anticipated being unable to get an erection, which made him so anxious that he avoided sex altogether. My clients do this all the time. Something doesn't go according to plan—when they are trying to conceive, when they are under pressure at work, when they've had too much to drink—and they realize for the first time that their bodies don't have an on-off switch. They feel out of control. I also told Shane that he had to banish the word *performance* from his vocabulary. A performance is one-way with one person on stage and someone else spectating. These are not feelings one should ever have during a sexual experience.

I explored Sydney's pregnancy and birth trauma. She hadn't processed her experience in therapy before, and it was clear the trauma was stuck in her body, manifesting itself through her attempt to micromanage everything her son came into contact with and affecting her ability to surrender to her own desire.

Yes, Shane and Sydney had a roof over their heads, but I felt that their metaphorical roof had caved in. Would they find a way to dance under the stars? I wanted to help them start on an individual level. We began a discussion about how to discover their innate ability to adapt.

DISCOVERING ADAPTABILITY WITHIN YOURSELF

Adaptability leads to confidence and courage, and confidence and courage in turn make it easier to adapt to new situations. But for many of us, this does not happen easily, let alone automatically. As we'll see in this section, people who are resilient tend to be in control of their responses rather than reactive to the world around them. Sydney tried to control her environment, and Shane tried to control his body. Instead, they needed to look internally at their own emotional experiences. I will explain how I helped them and how you can apply the same tools to yourself when life throws you curveballs. This is an important skill when it comes to keeping relationships and sex alive when life tries to get in the way.

Being flexible, as opposed to rigid, is a key skill for adapting to the unexpected. Award-winning Harvard Medical School psychologist Dr. Susan David describes this as *emotional agility*.[3] According to David, people who are emotionally agile learn to loosen up, stay calm, and live life with more intention. They make a choice about how to respond to their emotional warning systems. They are dynamic and demonstrate flexibility in adapting to our complex world. How many of you have had thoughts like *I don't want to feel anxious, I don't want to feel sad, I never want to get overwhelmed*, or *I don't want to have to overcome a problem*? She refers to these as *dead people's goals* because if you never want to experience them, you may as well be dead, she says. At the end of the day, setback and adversity are things we must be prepared to face. The more emotionally agile we are, the more easily we adapt in a way that keeps our lives feeling meaningful.

Many of us are guilty of defining ourselves by our problems, just as Shane had done. Rather than brushing off his inability to last very long as a one-off occurrence, he'd become so consumed by it that it shut him down from initiating anything at all. David encourages people to ask themselves, *But what else?* We tend to pigeonhole ourselves into a specific feeling or into a specific negative belief (i.e., *I'm not a good lover*), which makes us completely ignore other factors at play. Asking yourself things like *What else am I in this moment?* or *What do I have control over?* can expand our perspectives. Doing so helps us feel a sense of freedom and potential that we might not have otherwise tapped into. Had Shane acknowledged that in addition to losing his erection, he was also a wonderful husband and had plenty of experience being a passionate lover to Sydney, he may have continued to make love with her in ways that didn't require penile tumescence.

Shane and Sydney were fortunate to have gone through

life without much adversity. Shane was raised in a small town to parents who still loved each other after forty years. He grew up hunting and could skin a deer with his eyes closed. (Don't forget, I'm writing this from Texas!) He thought experiences like this had toughened him, but they hadn't prepared him for the kind of emotional adversity he faced with Sydney.

I sat with them at the next session, eager to explore their individual hang-ups in the context of a couple's session.

"Nothing humbled me more than becoming a father. I know I'm not the first man to feel that way, but I didn't expect it to take me out the way it did. This preoccupation with needing to provide more is driving me mad. On top of that, I can't even make love to my wife. What kind of man am I? It's no wonder she's uninterested in sex."

I explained to him how common it is for men to gain their sense of worth and esteem from work and sex. It's not uncommon for both areas to suffer if there are problems with one. I've worked with countless men who lose interest in sex or experience other sexual dysfunctions when there are issues at the office. On the flip side, I see men unable to focus at work until their sexual issues are resolved. I decided to apply Susan David's approach to see if it would help him look beyond the limitations he was so stuck on.

"Right now, you're totally focused on your erectile difficulty, and it's stopping you from initiating sex. I'm curious, when you think of making love to Sydney in the past, what do you think gave her the most pleasure?" This was my version of the *But what else?* question that David poses. I wanted to understand the other facets of their sexual relationship.

He thought for a moment. "There is no doubt we both enjoy the feeling of intercourse. Being connected in that way is very special. But in terms of physical pleasure, it's usual oral sex that helps her climax."

"Tell me why you assume that oral sex is just about physical pleasure for her and not emotional too," I pressed.

"I don't know. I don't have a good answer for you. I guess that is an assumption."

I turned my attention to his wife. "Sydney, can you describe what receiving oral sex is like for you? What, if anything, does it do for you emotionally?"

"I'm glad you're bringing this up," she started. "I regret stopping sex when he came quickly or giving up when he's been unable to get an erection. I guess I felt like it wasn't fair to keep going if he was having issues. But now—especially since having a kid—oral sex does a lot for me emotionally. First, he's very skilled." She smiled at him. He blushed. "Second, it's nice to have someone totally focused on my pleasure for once. Even though Devon is easier now than when he was a baby, it's still exhausting. I'm tired at the end of the day, but I have to rally so I can meet the needs of an energetic five-year-old. The idea of someone doing something just for me—for my pleasure—sounds divine."

I saw the light bulb turn on for Shane, but not before he turned it off again. "But, honey, maybe you wouldn't be so tired at the end of the day if you didn't have to work."

Sydney shook her head, exasperated. "Here we go again. I don't know how to get through to him that my work is also something that fills my cup. Yes, I'm tired at the end of the day, but in an accomplished and satisfactory way. He's hung up on this whole 'need to provide' thing."

I turned to Shane. "I'd like to talk about how you provide in a way that's not measured in dollars and cents. What other provisions do you think are meaningful to Sydney?"

"I haven't thought about that much. My dad worked, and my mom stayed home. I think it's just what was modeled for me."

"I wonder what Sydney would say." I turned to her.

She took a deep breath. "I think these types of gender roles are archaic. I don't want to sound harsh, but when he talks like this, it just makes him seem unevolved. It's a turnoff. I care more about his emotional availability to me and to our son. That's a more important foundation than how much money he brings home. It's our ability to work together as a team that will carry us through life's ups and downs. When I see him wrestling in the backyard with Devon or when he comes over to rub my neck after a long day—that's what does it for me. It's his attentiveness. Of course, the money isn't totally inconsequential. We both want financial security, but there's more to him than that. I fell in love with him in college when we were totally broke. I want that part of him back."

I looked at Shane and could see that her words were beginning to sink in.

"I guess I'd forgotten how meaningful everything else was to her," he said. "It's easy to lose sight of what's important."

It's easy to forget what counts when we find ourselves struggling in life. One of the books I go back to time and again is *Man's Search for Meaning* by Viktor Frankl. He wrote the book after surviving life in a concentration camp and later became known as one of the fathers of positive psychology (the branch of psychology that flow is nestled in). Frankl posed that life isn't about a quest for pleasure or power but rather a quest for meaning. Think back to the last chapter when we explored how to make sex more meaningful and how doing so can enhance satisfaction and deepen intimacy. Frankl reminds us that you can't control what happens to you in life, but you can control how you respond. Frankl's ability to psychologically persevere in what can only be thought of as hell on earth can serve as a reminder to all of us that we can do better than letting our problems get the best of us. You have to ask yourself—are you the kind of person who is going to let adversity kill your sex life (sex being one of the most life-affirming experiences we have), or will Frankl's words ring through your head—that "the salvation of man is through love and in love"?[4]

What distinguishes someone who grows from negative events from someone who continues to suffer? Shane had started to make sense of his own issues, but Sydney was still stuck in her own anxiety. I was reminded of social psychologist Eranda Jayawickreme's work on trauma.[5] Rather than studying post-traumatic stress, he turned his attention to post-traumatic *growth*. Jayawickreme grew up in Sri Lanka, a brutal civil war the backdrop of his youth. Terrible violence became normalized. He moved to the United States not long before 9/11 and describes a light bulb moment upon assessing his reaction to the events of that day. Instead of experiencing horror, he felt detached and indifferent. He realized that despite thinking he was stronger from what he'd witnessed in Sri Lanka, he wasn't; he was anesthetized. *How could feelings of numbness and apathy represent healthy psychological growth?* he wondered. Some people think hardness *is* strength, but Jayawickreme wasn't convinced.

And I agree. We can't fully thrive when we are emotionally anesthetized. Jayawickreme began examining philosophical, theological, and psychological texts to uncover what he could about the nature of suffering and how it impacts people. He wanted to understand what made some people adapt (and thrive) despite suffering versus what made others feel stuck. The key difference, he discovered, is how we make sense of our trauma. In other words, it's about how we reflect on our own suffering.[6] Experiencing trauma alone, it turns out, isn't enough to build character and wisdom. Reflection and insight are keys to turning adversity into adaptability.

How can we use adversity to build character and resourcefulness so that we can more effectively adapt to life's curveballs? Jayawickreme assessed the impact of two fundamental responses to trauma—how you control the environment around you (primary control) and how you control your response to the trauma (secondary control).[7] He found that people who focus on controlling their immediate surroundings experience more positive emotions, whereas people who focus on controlling their personal response experience greater life satisfaction. There are benefits to both, but as a society, we've become overly reliant on primary control. Unhappy with a relationship? Open an app and find a new one. Not fully satisfied with your purchase? Return it within thirty days, shipping included. Dinner not turn out quite right? No worries, just run to the fast-food chain around the corner. Penis not working? Pop a little blue pill. But sometimes we can't fix our lives quite so easily. When we come to these roadblocks and there is no primary fix, it's tempting to turn to frustration instead of adaptability. How do we instead shift our response (secondary control) and look for solutions within ourselves?

I thought about Sydney, who had yet to process her traumatic birth and first year as a mother of a colicky baby. She'd turned to external control of her environment rather than internal understanding of her own emotional reaction. The organic cucumbers lovingly cut into dinosaur shapes, the mommy-and-me pajama sets, the hour-long bedtime routine that started at 7:30 sharp, the cleaning products she made from lemon juice and vinegar—was this the behavior of a loving mother, or was it a futile attempt to mask her internal emotional turmoil? Yes, these things gave her pleasure, but how satisfied were they really making her?

Like Shane, she was fortunate in that she'd had a rather uneventful childhood. The birth of Devon was the first major trauma she'd experienced. I asked her to tell me about the experience. She choked back sobs as she described the rush to the hospital, the look on the nurse's face when she checked the baby's heart rate, the doctors running into the hospital room, how blue Devon looked when he first came out.

"I've never felt more out of control in my life. Doing these things for Devon now has helped me regain a sense of control I didn't have when he first came into this world."

"I completely get that," I told her. "But I also wonder how in 'control' you really are versus how much you've let the negative experience control you." She looked at me quizzically. "Think back to how you described sex with Shane in the early days. I got the sense that it was carefree. You used the words *fun* and *spontaneous*. And I caught a glimpse of that when I first started with you. I detected a playfulness between the two of you. But rather than holding on to that part of yourself despite what you went through, you've become tangled in a web of routines and perfection. When you think of everything you do for Devon, what emotions and sensations do you notice in your body?"

She closed her eyes. "I feel love and warmth, but I also feel a tightness in my chest. My muscles get tense."

I looked at her with compassion. "That's what I'm talking about. It's anxiety driving you, not love alone. None of the things you're doing are 'wrong.' I'm not saying you should stop making organic cleaning products if that's important to you, but I want to see where there might be space for more flexibility. How would it feel, for example, if the three of you enjoyed an evening out past 7:30 if the weather was particularly nice? This is internal control. It's noticing the urge to live life with rigidity and instead find pockets of flexibility that might make your life more meaningful. I'd be willing to bet the memory of a late-summer stroll under a cotton-candy sky sticks with you more than the countless bedtime routines you're accustomed to. You can do both. It's about integration, not subjugation."

In the end, it turns out the "what doesn't kill you makes you stronger" mantra is a bit overly simplistic; people who effectively process their trauma aren't necessarily stronger, they are just able to feel the spectrum of their emotions in more complex ways. Jayawickreme and his colleagues are working on developing interventions for people who have experienced adversity. They are teaching people to use setbacks as opportunities to reflect on their core values and see them as a chance to double down on how they want to live their lives. Remember Susan David's question—*But what else?* It's important to remember that whatever problems we are facing on the surface are not always the whole issue; Shane's erectile issues, for example, were emblematic of a deeper emotional need. If we are to fully adapt when we have a problem, we must look at the full, if not complex, picture.

Take a moment to reflect on a setback you've experienced in your life. In the following exercise, consider what you've learned about overcoming adversity, and think about how you might adapt to handle the situation differently.

Learning from Our Obstacles

Think of a setback from your past. Try to identify something that really knocked you off your feet.

What was the incident?
What was the emotional/physical effect on you?
How did it make you think about yourself / others / the world?

Now imagine applying skills in resilience, emotional agility, and adaptability to that incident. Even if the negative outcome was the same, the overall *effect* on you could be different.

What lessons can you learn from your experience?
How might your thoughts/feelings about yourself change?
How might that change affect your behavior now?

People who adapt effectively can hold space for the complexity of both the good and the bad that come from adversity. The same holds true in relationships, which is where we are headed next.

CREATING ADAPTABILITY IN YOUR RELATIONSHIP

Adaptability is key to a long-term relationship that is both meaningful and filled with happiness. Relationships are about more than enjoying the day-to-day—though that is important, as well. Couples should also prepare for unexpected speed bumps. Perhaps you'll have to move unexpectedly or one of you will lose your job. Maybe someone in the family becomes seriously ill. How couples wade through the rough waters of a relationship can make or break it. As much as we might crave stability and predictability in our relationships, change is inevitable. Change may happen outside the relationship, forcing the couple to adjust, or internally if one or both people in the relationship grow or change as individuals. While couples should learn to apply the philosophies described in the previous section to their relationship, there are a few principles that speak specifically to relationship adaptability—integrity, forgiveness, and social support.

Integrity

Most people see the word *integrity* and think about honor. Obviously, being an honorable person is important for the health of the relationship. The health of our relationships will suffer if we fail to follow through on our commitments and take responsibility for our mistakes. But I like to think of integrity a little bit differently. Integrity is also about wholeness. It's about being complete and undivided. It's about strength. The integrity of a lock, for instance, determines how secure your home is. In my sessions with clients, I often see adversity decrease the integrity of the relationship. Shane and Sydney's sex life, for instance, lost its integrity when it became dependent on the quality of his erection. Only when they shifted their focus to view sex more holistically did Sydney and Shane begin to regain wholeness, as we'll see laid out in a later section.

We can maintain relationship integrity by being nurturing of our partnerships and of each other's need to grow. Think of what a plant needs to stay healthy and strong—sunshine, water, and good soil. An unhealthy plant cannot weather a storm. A healthy plant, by contrast, may lose a few leaves through the storm, but its roots stay firm and new leaves eventually grow. A healthy relationship can be thought of like a plant that is continuously growing and evolving. If we fail to nurture a plant the way it needs, it will eventually die. Without the integrity needed to grow and adapt to change, our relationships will calcify. There will invariably be factors that threaten the integrity or wholeness of a relationship, but a strong relationship has the tools it needs to rebalance harmony and homeostasis, even if that means the relationship looks a bit different from the way it did prior to the change.

I love what therapist and author Terrence Real says about harmony in relationships: "A good relationship is a relationship that survives the whole [cycle]. A good relationship is a relationship that moves from harmony to disharmony and doesn't get stuck there but moves from disharmony back into repair. That's where the skills come in."[8] You cannot overcome hardship without relational integrity.

This theme came up repeatedly in my research. Two of my participants, Landon and Marissa, described the splinter in their relationship when Landon made the choice to cut ties with his alcoholic brother. Marissa said, "For about eighteen months, it felt like he cut ties off with me along with his brother. His personality changed. I knew he was angry and sad about what he was going through, but I felt like I couldn't get through to him. He was so distant. We rarely had sex. With the help of a good couples' therapist, we gradually worked to rebuild our relationship alongside Landon reclaiming his identity apart from his relationship with his brother. He needed to figure out how to be whole again before our relationship—and our sex life—could be whole too."

Jacob and Martin's relationship suffered as they struggled to adapt to their son's autism diagnosis. "It was an incredibly challenging time," Jacob said. "At the time of his diagnosis, we were both working crazy hours. We had good help, but obviously felt pulled to spend more time with him. He needed us. We felt broken and stretched too thin. We were constantly snapping at each other, which didn't help at all with the monstrous level of stress we were under. We finally sat down and reassessed what was really important to us. We had to shift our values and priorities if we were going to adapt and survive this as a family. We made some significant changes, but today, we are happier than ever."

When you feel like you and your partner are struggling to adapt to change, spend some time reassessing your relationship value system and see how doing so helps you find relationship integrity.

Relationship Values

It's easier to navigate the ebbs and flows of life when you feel like you and your partner can work as a team. Part of that is periodically checking in with each other on values and beliefs.

It's also helpful to think about how important your stance is on any given issue. For example, your partner may feel very strongly about where you live, but that may not be as important to you. By comparing notes on how strongly you feel about various issues, you can maintain relational integrity when faced with an unexpected challenge.

You Try It:
Write a sentence or two on your thoughts and feelings regarding each value. Then rank them on a scale of its importance, with 0 being unimportant and 10 being the most important. Use your responses to open a discussion with your partner. Talk specifically about what strategies you might employ if something gets in the way of your value.

VALUE	THOUGHTS	IMPORTANCE (0–10)
Spending time together		
Spending time alone		
Spending time with family		
Spending time with friends		
Employment		
Work-life balance		
Where / how you live		
Travel and vacations		
Parenting		
Health and fitness		
Mental health / counseling		
Hobbies		
Sex		
Religion / spirituality		

Every couple needs to periodically consider what they need to maintain a sense of integrity, or wholeness, in their relationship. Reassessing your relationship values can help you prioritize what's important in the face of anticipated or unanticipated adversity. It's normal for values to change as the relationship evolves, which is why periodically discussing them with your partner can be so helpful.

Personal integrity, or wholeness, is also an important piece of relationship wholeness. Our relationships with others (as we'll see in our discussion on social support) help us become more whole (i.e., maintain more individual integrity) without relying on our partners to do so. The more whole we are, the more we bring to the bedroom. Sex suffers when we show up fragmented and when we rely too much on our partners to "make us whole."

I remember swooning as a teenager when Jerry (played by Tom Cruise) tearfully professed his love to Dorothy (played by Renée Zellweger) in *Jerry Maguire*. He looks deeply and passionately into her eyes and declares, "You complete me." The teenage me longed for a love like that. The adult me cringes. For when we rely on our romantic partners to be our everything, to complete us, to make us whole, we snuff the flame of desire.

I will caveat this with the sentiment that there is too much of an emphasis on individualism, especially in the West. I don't want you to read this and leave with the idea that we must be in perfect order before having a healthy relationship. That is not what I am saying. In fact, I believe that relationships can be a wonderful source of healing and personal growth. My word of caution is that you don't neglect vital parts of yourself as you enter into a relationship with another.

Everything that makes you who you are is going to come through as part of your erotic identity. If you're not whole, if you've disconnected from important, vital parts of yourself, you're limiting your capacity for full sexual expression.

Forgiveness

Forgiveness is a complicated component of healing and growth. What is the relationship between forgiving and forgetting? Does forgiveness mean to acquiesce? Is it possible to move forward without forgiveness? What is the relationship between power and forgiveness? What are the limits of forgiveness?

At its core, forgiveness means *to absolve, to let go, and to cease to feel resentment against.* Inherent in this definition is both the relational and personal element of forgiveness—relational in the sense you are absolving someone of the wrongs they have done, and personal in the sense you are letting go of anger you may still hold. It is important to distinguish between forgiveness and trust. As my friend and colleague Beth Christopherson says, "Forgiveness heals the individual, but trust heals the relationship." Reestablishing trust requires making any necessary behavioral changes while also showing up emotionally for your partner. And so, when a couple is faced with a conflict only to find that the anger or resentment they feel is so great that adapting and moving forward seems impossible, there is only one solution: they must learn to forgive and build trust once more (at least if they choose to stay).

All too often, conflict results in resentment instead of

forgiveness, and resentment is a potent precursor for sexual disconnect. Many of the couples I spoke with who felt they'd maintained an amazing sex life over the long haul included forgiveness as part of their journey. My research participant Miriam described the process of forgiving her husband for making a large investment without consulting her. It wasn't until she let go of her anger toward him that she was able to make love to him again. Another participant, Quinn, described how forgiveness played a role in their sexuality journey. Their parents didn't initially accept their gender identity. It wasn't until they were able to let go of the hurt they still harbored that they were able to surrender to their own erotic pleasure, thereby adapting and fully leaning into their new sense of self.

Forgiveness can be scary. It can feel like you're surrendering power by remitting someone for how they've wronged you. I see many of my clients default to anger because they confuse it with power. Anger makes us feel powerful, at least in the moment, but over time, it festers, having the opposite effect. It can be tempting to seek revenge, because who wants to be alone in their pain and suffering? But revenge doesn't get us anywhere; in fact, it only makes things worse.[9] Forgiveness has important health benefits, including increased optimism, lower rates of anxiety and depression, and better cardiovascular health.[10] In short, it feels good to let go, and doing so helps us move on with life. Most important, forgiveness helps us adapt more easily. We can't move forward if we are still holding on to something from the past.

Forgiveness, of course, has its limits. Like it or not,

adult romantic love is conditional. Someone in an abusive relationship should not continue to absolve the abuser of their offenses. At some point, the abuser will need to be held accountable and the relationship should end. Internal forgiveness (letting go of resentment and pain) may be the only component of forgiveness in a situation like this. I like the following exercise for all kinds of forgiveness, but especially for times when forgiveness needs to happen internally.

Forgiveness to Move Forward

Is there something you need to forgive? If you're holding on to resentment about something from the past, it will make it harder to overcome challenges that may arise in the future.

You Try It:

1. Identify something you're holding resentment about.

2. Cut strips of paper. Write down things from the past, present, and future that you need to let go of. For instance, something from the past might be, "Your distance during my miscarriage." Something from the present might be, "The lingering resentment I still hold from it." Something from the future might be, "My expectation that you handle stress the same way I do."

3. One by one, say goodbye to each item you wrote down on your strips of paper. I suggest doing so ritualistically. For instance, you might throw them into the fireplace, drop them into a stream of running water, or send them into the sky tied to a balloon.

Releasing pain creates space, which makes it easier to move forward with love and connection. Forgiveness can be challenging without people around to help us through the process. Social support, as we'll see, plays a big role in helping couples adapt to change.

Social Support

One of the first questions I ask clients is about their support systems. Integrity and forgiveness (and thus adaptability) are easier when we have people around who can support us through hard times. As Esther Perel famously said in her TED Talk, "We come to one person, and we basically are asking them to give us what once an entire village used to provide."[11] We expect so much more out of our romantic relationships than ever before. Expecting everything out of one person can put too much pressure on the relationship, making it more prone to snap. Pressure, not surprisingly, is one of the fastest things to kill desire. When we draw too much out of our partners, they have nothing left to give us in the erotic realm.

Alas, we don't live in villages anymore. In the United States, we are often spread out, not just geographically but socially and emotionally. Many of our neighbors are transient or disconnected from one another. It's hard to establish a community whether in a suburb, where there are fewer gathering places, or in a city, where we are so densely packed that it's overwhelming to interface with everyone. It's harder than ever to establish social bonds reminiscent of the age-old village.

Social support anchors us. People who have a strong social support network have lower rates of depression, better overall health, and higher life satisfaction.[12] People with wide social networks also find it easier to overcome adversity. Assess your social support with the following exercise.

Your Social Support System

We expect more out of our romantic relationships than ever before. But expecting our partners to be our lovers, our best friends, our birth partners, our financial partners, our co-parents, our strongest supporters, our shoulders to cry on, our partners in crime, the people we share hobbies with, our intellectual equals, our (you get the idea) can put an enormous amount of pressure on a relationship. One of the key factors that resilient people share is a strong social support system, a rich resource into which they can tap when life feels overwhelming.

You Try It:

Make a list of people, groups, or organizations that you consider to be a part of your social support system. Write down what you get from each source of support.

SOURCE OF SUPPORT	WHAT IT GIVES ME

I discussed social support with Shane and Sydney.

"Part of the reason I get so frustrated with Shane when he talks about me quitting work is because I value the relationships I have with my colleagues. We are a family in a way. I don't want to give that up."

Shane nodded in understanding. I explained to him that I encourage the couples I work with to have friends outside their romantic relationships.

"There is an emphasis on date nights," I began, "and while the importance of quality time as a couple should not be underestimated, quality time with people outside the relationship is a close second."

It seemed to sink in for Shane. He admitted he'd feel lousy if he had to give up his weekly basketball game with his college buddies.

"Tell me more about what that weekly game does for you," I pressed.

"I get it," he said. "It's more than a social and physical outlet for me. It makes the worries of my day seem, well, less worrisome."

"Exactly," I said. "Which, in effect, makes it easier to cope with any little adversities you may have experienced that day. It helps you adapt. The same is true for Sydney's support system at the design firm."

Shane and Sydney were beginning to step out of the rut they were in as individuals and within their relationship. They were ready to apply everything they'd learned to their sex life.

CULTIVATING ADAPTABILITY IN EROTICISM

Adaptability is arguably the most important skill in helping you cultivate a sexual experience that stands the test of time. The sex you have during the honeymoon phase of the relationship versus twenty years in—the love you make while trying to conceive versus while you or your partner are pregnant and in the postpartum period, the quickie you sneak with young kids in the house or with teenagers up late at night—is all going to be different. The sex you have when you're empty nesters, while on vacation, when you're energized, sleep-deprived, particularly stressed, or physically or emotionally injured, it will all be different. The key to keeping it hot during all these phases of life and circumstances is to be flexible about the kind of sex you're having.

If you pick a sexual script, which can be thought of as your sexual recipe, and stick with it for your whole partnership, you're going to feel disappointed. To maintain eroticism in long-term relationships, it is essential to be open and nonjudgmental to whatever happens during a sexual encounter. Things happen during sex that we don't expect. Like Shane, your body may not function the way you're accustomed to it functioning. Your partner may spring a new position or technique on you that momentarily takes you off guard. You may make an unintended sound. It is vital that we don't let things like this derail an otherwise great sexual encounter. We need to know how to deal with the unplanned if we are to continue to enjoy our sexual experiences for the long haul.

There is an animated video by sex educator Karen B. K. Chan titled *Sex as a Jam Session*.[13] A musical jam session happens when a group of musicians comes together to play music that isn't planned. Some of the most incredible instrumentals happen when musicians throw their music books out the window and instead flow with whatever happens as they jam out. Chan encourages couples to approach sex the same way. This is something Nolan and Grace, a couple who participated in my research study, relayed to me during one of our sessions. "We view our sex as very fluid, and I think that's one of the things that makes it so great. Our sex doesn't have a beginning, middle, and end. It's an energy that's always there between us. What happens with our bodies just depends on where we jump in. Getting handsy in the middle of the night might lead to early-morning sex, which makes us feel connected. But we don't make out during morning sex because of, well, morning breath, so then we usually spend more time kissing before falling asleep later that night. We are both open-minded, which makes it easy to stay on the same page. We are aligned. Some things we talk about doing, and other things happen organically, in the moment."

It is more difficult to adapt to the unexpected if the sex you're having follows the same choreography each time. Besides, sex that follows the same script eventually gets boring. Instead, approaching sex with an open mind helps retain fluidity (and excitement) much like a stream that effortlessly flows around rocks that may be in its path.

In addition to being flexible to what happens or doesn't happen in the moment, it's also important to adapt to evolving preferences and desires. I've worked with countless couples who, at a certain point in the relationship, decide there is a new aspect of their sexuality that they want to explore.

Maybe they read something in erotica, see something in a movie, or overhear a friend share a detail that sounds exciting. There is comfort in familiarity and predictability, but just as our literal taste buds change over time, so do many people's sexual tastes. So, how do we handle it when our partners suddenly want to switch things up?

Do you remember how we talked about fixed versus growth mindsets in the previous chapter? Researchers have expanded on these concepts to investigate the difference between couples who have *sexual growth beliefs* and couples who have *sexual destiny beliefs*.[14] People who hold sexual destiny beliefs think a good sex life happens as the result of finding the right partner, but they end up struggling more when sexual or relationship challenges arise. People who endorse sexual growth beliefs, however, know that satisfying sexual relationships require effort to maintain. As a result, they tend to report higher sexual, relationship, and personal well-being even when faced with a sexual challenge. These folks are also more motivated to meet a partner's needs than folks who hold sexual destiny beliefs. In other words, they are more open to going with the flow, or adapting, to when there is a sexual challenge or when their partners want to try something new. At the end of the day, they understand that pleasure is not automatic, nor is it set.

Just as we have the right to pursue happiness, we have the right to pursue pleasure. It's not going to magically manifest. I encourage my clients to think of cultivating great sex the way they would think of any other pleasure in life. When we want something badly enough, we will do just about anything to get it. That means great sex then becomes about *intention*. Rather than wasting your time wishing it came automatically like it did in a honeymoon phase, take a moment and consider how your current stage in life might be an opportunity for growth and new connection. Call me romantic, but I think there is something far more special about intentionally cultivating great sex as opposed to passively waiting for it to show up on your doorstep (or in your bed, for that matter). Doing so creates a passion and intensity that far exceeds what you felt in the early days. With the right tools, sex can be an incredible gateway for emotional, psychological, and spiritual growth, both as an individual and within your relationship—that is, *if* you maintain a growth mindset and a willingness to adapt to change.

One way to ensure we enjoy fulfilling sex in long-term relationships is to expand our understanding of sexual desire. It's hard to adapt to change, after all, when our understanding of sexuality is narrow or when we are unaware of our options. Human sexual response was originally thought of as linear—first we experience sexual desire, then physical arousal, then orgasm.[15] But now we know that this is not how many people experience desire. The original models considered only the physiological changes that happen as part of sexual response, but modern sexologists realized that emotional and psychological changes are important too, especially for women. Things like trust, intimacy, pleasure, communication, and affection all play a role in how we experience desire. Thankfully, a new circular model was created. This model incorporates the importance of emotional closeness and sexual satisfaction as considerations for sexual desire and response. In other words, many people need to feel emotionally close to their partners *and* experience a little bit of sexual arousal *before* they notice a desire for sex. We refer to this as *responsive sexual desire*. Many people, particularly women, notice they engage in sex from a place of neutrality rather than from a rip-off-my-clothes-right-now state of mind. Desire then emerges as arousal builds. Assuming the sex is good and leaves you not just physically satisfied but also emotionally connected, you're more likely to experience spontaneous sexual desire sometimes too, like the original model proposed.

This is important for several reasons. First, when you're in the honeymoon stage of the relationship, it may feel like everything sexual happens easily, automatically, and spontaneously. Six to eighteen months into the relationship, however, when the neurochemical high subsides and the rose-colored glasses come off, it may not feel like desire happens as automatically. This can lead many people to think they have low desire, when in fact, all the ingredients are still there; couples just have to learn how to work with them in a new way. This is where curiosity (explained in the previous chapter) and adaptability come into play. In the absence of spontaneous, mind-blowing sex, you and your partner must learn to adapt to the inevitable changes that come with a long-term relationship. Great sex then becomes about cultivation, creation, and intention.

Planned Versus Spontaneous Sex

Once you get behind the idea that desire doesn't always emerge spontaneously, you can begin to understand how beneficial it is to plan sex. Stay with me for this. My clients are stubborn about this one, but making a plan—being conscious and intentional—is the best way to navigate (i.e., adapt) around everything else pulling for your attention. I tense when I broach the topic of planning sex because I know the response I'm going to get—an eye roll, a huff, a closing-argument-style defense as to why spontaneous sex is better. But plainly stated, we grossly underestimate the beauty and pleasure of planned sex. Planned sex can be better; in fact, it usually is.

The element of surprise within the confines of an emotionally safe relationship is the perfect cocktail for optimal sex. But what is the best way to create adventure when we are making plans? I think we can do both at the same time. Spontaneity is loads of fun. The coquettish feel of *I didn't see that coming* mixed with the rush and passion of feeling equally invested in the encounter is thrilling. But we must remember, as Emily Nagoski reminds us in *Come As You Are*, even the most spontaneous-feeling encounters most likely have an element of planning.[16] Think sex is spontaneous when you're on vacation? Think again. You selected a romantic destination, booked a room with a good view, put in for PTO months in advance, and went shopping for a new vacation outfit. Whether spoken or unspoken, a lot of planning went into creating the perfect context for "spontaneous" sex to happen.

A lot of people have this idea that sex isn't good unless it happens spontaneously. The faster you get over that idea, the better off you are. When you're in a long-term relationship with a million commitments, it's going to be hard to count on good sex happening completely spontaneously. Doing so will limit the opportunity you have to experience the full spectrum of erotic pleasure.

Here's what I remind couples when it comes to planning sex:

1. When you were dating, you were planning it. You just didn't call it that. You called it "I'll pick you up on Saturday night." But everybody knew what was going down at the end of the night, and there was plenty of planning and preparation that went into that—personal grooming, careful outfit selection, thoughtfulness, and buckets of excited anticipation.

2. Use the word *plan* as opposed to *schedule*. *Planning* has a more positive connotation. You plan a party or lunch with a friend. You schedule a visit to the dentist or a meeting with your CPA.

3. Just because you plan *when* doesn't mean you have to plan *what*. You can throw in a little spontaneity about what you do even if you planned for the when.

4. Make planned sex your plan B as opposed to your plan A. Be sure to leave space for spontaneous encounters in between planned ones. The planned sex can be thought of as a fallback plan.

5. Use planned sex as an opportunity to step further outside the box than you would if you relied solely on in-the-moment exploration. You can only push your limits if everyone is crystal clear about what those limits and desires are. Talk to any kinky couple and they will excitedly tell you the extent to which they plan their escapades.

6. Remember that you can always cancel your plans. Forcing yourself to do something just because it's on the calendar never feels good, especially when it comes to sex. If you find that you just can't get in the right headspace, if you don't feel good, if you're

too tired, and so on, you always have the right to re-schedule.

Remember—anything good takes planning, practice, intention, and commitment. Extraordinary lovers know this and apply it to sex. They describe preparing the environment, themselves, and the relationship and making sure they have enough time.[17] We make plans for just about anything else that is important to us. Why not take the same approach when it comes to sex?

I encouraged Shane and Sydney to start carving out time to connect erotically.

"No way I'll be able to get an erection if it's planned!" Shane exclaimed.

I'd heard this reaction a million times before. "Trust me on this one," I told him. "In fact, I think it's better that you plan *not* to get an erection. Don't even think about it. Sydney mentioned how wonderful it would be to be the sole receiver of pleasure every now and then. Why don't you try using the time to focus on her?"

He looked at me with hesitation.

Sydney looked at me with excitement, but then added, "I feel like I'll experience pressure to get in the mood if I know it's coming."

"Try not to worry about that too much right now," I told her. I explained how she could assess whether she's entering their time together from a place of neutrality versus true disinterest. "If you're feeling neutral and at least open to connection, I want you to go for it. I want this to be a first step in broadening your sexual script."

Flipping Your Sexual Script

Not only do we need to more fully understand the different ways desire manifests and accept the fact that planned sex can be great sex, we also need to change our definition of what "sex" is. Most people, especially heterosexual couples, use erections and orgasms as a barometer to measure the quality of sex. That's not to say those aren't wonderful components of sex, but we shouldn't think of them as the end all, be all.

In fact, the majority of participants in Dr. Peggy Kleinplatz's research reported that intercourse was inconsequential for an optimal sexual experience.[18] One of her subjects said, "There needs to be a crossing of the boundary in a physical way but it doesn't have to be necessarily going inside someone. It can be going between them or wrapping around them. It's a . . . blurring of the strict boundaries, but it doesn't have to include [penetration]."

What ends up happening is that people fall into a routine, or what I like to refer to as a *sexual script*. First, they do this, then that, and before you know it, they're having sex that feels mundane and boring. You're not going to feel inspired to adapt to inevitable challenges (like navigating erectile dysfunction or having to adjust positions because of a bad hip) if you're already bored with your sex life. I encourage my clients to think about how they may rewrite their sexual scripts. The more they practice that in advance of any potential problems that arise, the more primed they'll be to adapt to the changes that are inevitably going to come.

By now, you know that Sydney and Shane had fallen into the trap of a rigid, limited sexual script. It had been fun and spontaneous once upon a time, but only if the core ingredients were there (i.e., his erection). When Shane struggled to get an erection, he and Sydney stopped having sex as opposed to opening up a cookbook to see what other yummy recipes may be waiting to be whipped up. I wanted to work with them to find ways of expanding their sexual repertoire so that their pleasure didn't hinge on his penis.

I explained to Sydney and Shane that I wanted to broaden the way they thought about sex and gave them the following exercise to get the ball rolling.

Flip Your Sexual Script

It's important to know that the sex you share over the course of a long-term relationship is going to evolve. The list of factors that can potentially affect the way in which you have sex goes on and on.

Because sex is so dynamic, it is important to remain flexible to whatever happens, yet many couples get locked into one sexual script—that is, they fall into a routine for the way they expect sex to play out. When we become too locked in our scripts, our rigidity increases and our ability to be flexible to changes in sexuality diminishes.

This exercise encourages you to flip the script.

You Try It:

In the first column, write down the steps you typically follow when you have sex. For most people, it goes—undress, kiss, genital stimulation, intercourse, orgasm, done.

In the second column, imagine that your partner has a wrist fracture in their dominant hand. What modifications would you make? How can you work around their limitation to keep sex fun and exciting?

In the third column, imagine one of you is struggling with a sexual dysfunction. Perhaps your partner has an off night and just can't get an erection. Or perhaps you went on a long bike ride and vaginal penetration feels like it would be too uncomfortable. How can you create an enjoyable sexual encounter that doesn't include intercourse?

In the fourth column, simply imagine a variation in the way you have sex. If your partner typically climaxes first, imagine the steps you'd have to take for you to come first. If you typically initiate, write down how it would feel for your partner to initiate.

CURRENT SCRIPT	PHYSICAL LIMITATION	SEXUAL LIMITATION	ALTERNATIVE SCRIPT

Shane and Sydney agreed to use their first few planned nights to focus on her pleasure. Perhaps not surprisingly, since Shane didn't go into the experience with the goal of getting an erection, he ended up getting an erection. He came quickly the first couple of times they were together, but they didn't end the experience with his climax. Instead, they used their time to hold, caress, and explore each other's bodies. Sydney even ended up having more than one orgasm on a few of these occasions. Eventually, a few months later, as their anxiety reduced and they discovered a new and improved rhythm as a couple, Shane regained his ejaculatory control. In my final session with them, they reported great joy over their newfound ability to maintain a sense of flexibility and openness as parents, within their relationship, and in their sex life. They had discovered the delights of sexual fluidity and were no longer beholden to Shane's erection or Sydney's orgasm. They relished in the pleasure of sharing each other's bodies, no matter what happened during each encounter.

Creating a new script is hard. We certainly don't see it happening in media. In films and TV, sex always appears to be spontaneous. You rarely see foreplay. You see couples having simultaneous orgasms like it's the norm, and then we wonder why our sex doesn't look like that. But Hollywood sex, if nothing else, is scripted. You don't see couples navigating sexual challenges, cleaning up the wet spot, or laughing together over a funny sound. When we diminish sex to what's happening physically with the body and further reduce it to intercourse alone, we shrink our erotic potential. Adaptive couples who think outside the box find that they are able to maintain intense, meaningful sex despite physical limitations or even chronic illness.

Experiencing sex as a jam session, widening your definition of sex, and being intentional about making sex pleasurable no matter what's happening in the background of life will help you experience vastly more meaningful sex.

If you're reading this and feeling worried because a lot of times you have sex for the sake of the relationship despite not being in the mood, you can exhale. Most enjoyable experiences begin as a combination of intrinsic and extrinsic reward. You may start trying to improve your sex life because you see doing so as beneficial to the relationship (extrinsic), but over time, as your own pleasure increases, the sexual experience will become intrinsically rewarding too (intrinsic). Most fun activities are not naturally or automatically intrinsically rewarding. Think of the first time you went skiing or sat in front of a chessboard. You had to be intentional about it until it became fun.

The more intrinsically motivated sex is, the more likely it will become something that is, as Csikszentmihalyi describes, *autotelic*. The word *autotelic* comes from the Greek words *auto*, meaning "self," and *telos*, meaning "goal." In other words, you do something for the sake of doing it, because doing so is intrinsically rewarding. Experiences that are autotelic in nature set us up to experience flow. When you're engaged in an activity that is intrinsically rewarding, you're doing it because the activity itself is the reward and not some future benefit. Take fishing. Someone who fishes because they need to eat is fishing for an extrinsic reward. Someone who fishes because they enjoy the experience of fishing is fishing for an intrinsic reward. Catching a fish and frying it up for dinner are added benefits to the joy of a few hours sitting at the end of the dock on a serene lake with a rod in hand. When you approach sex with a similar mindset, you are more likely to experience pleasure, connect, and have fun.

This theme came up among my research participants as well. Two people stood out for their stories about having sex despite chronic pain, one from cancer and one from chronic pancreatitis. They were both completely invested in having sex for the pleasure of sex itself. In both cases, it gave them a break from their physical and emotional pain.

I wanted Sydney and Shane to think about it in the same way. They had gone from passionate lovemaking in the early days to awkwardly fumbling their way through sex, completely forgetting why they were doing it to begin with. It wasn't until they learned to discover each other in new ways and prioritize it the way they once had that the experience again became intrinsically rewarding and mutually pleasurable.

We are fed the idea that sex isn't good unless it's easy and spontaneous. This mindset hinders our ability to navigate the unknowns and adapt to change. I hope that after reading this chapter, you'll find the courage within yourself to think outside the box. My wish for you is to remember that anything worth doing takes work. That includes sex. You'll find that life is more meaningful when you view hurdles as opportunities to grow and learn something new about yourself and your relationship. When you're willing to take personal, relationship, and even sexual risks (as we discussed in the previous chapter), you'll discover a newfound confidence. As an added bonus, you'll find that intimacy in your relationship deepens, creating an intensity you didn't even realize was there, which is where we're headed next.

4

THE INTENSITY OF VULNERABILITY

When you're soarin' through the air
I'll be your solid ground.
—"When You Come Back Down" by Nickel Creek

It amazes me how many of my clients report feeling completely terrified to do something as "simple" as make eye contact during sex. The exhilarating feeling of having the freedom to strip away all pretense, bare your soul, reveal parts of your psyche unknown to others, and even act on primal impulse is electrifyingly erotic. This action transports us to one of the most powerful yet *vulnerable* spaces in which we can exist. My clients Darius and Iman, like many people I've worked with over the years, struggled with this.

It was my second session with Darius and Iman, a married couple in their midthirties who came to see me to address the gradual decline in Darius's desire for intimacy over the past three years. Iman was concerned. She thought she and Darius had an amazing chemistry when they'd gotten together four years prior, and she couldn't understand why he'd gradually pulled away. He insisted it was nothing, that he was just busy with work. Three years earlier, around the time his desire began to wane, he'd taken on a new job as an energy trader. The hours were long, and the work was intense. He felt tapped out at the end of the day. To make matters worse, he resented Iman's persistence, and she resented the way he constantly rebuffed her. They were starting to grow distant.

In the previous year, they'd had sex fewer than a dozen times, and it was lackluster when they did. Darius pulled away quickly, leaving Iman feeling used. This was confusing because she *knew* he loved her, but he, for some reason unbeknownst to her, didn't seem able to express it anymore when they made love. This was a stark contrast to sex in the early days, when she felt totally devoured and enveloped by him, when he looked at her with energy and vitality.

Darius began the session defensively. "Iman, you know how much this job means to me. I'm doing the best I can to be a good husband to you, but it doesn't seem good enough."

She looked at me and shook her head. "I just don't buy it," she said. "Look, I get it—the new job takes a lot out of him, but I know Darius. Something else is going on. He has a tell. Sometimes when I ask him how his day was, he answers that it was fine, but I catch a subtle change in the pitch of his voice. I check the markets, and I know his day was anything but fine. I appreciate that he's trying to shield me from the ups and downs of his work. We want to have a baby, and I know he's trying to keep my stress levels down, but he gets the same pitch when I push him about sex. I feel like he hardly looks at me anymore when we make love. It's like he's tuning me out. I just know there is something he's not telling me." She paused. "Can I tell her the other thing?"

Darius stiffened and nodded quickly.

Iman looked at me. "I've walked in on him masturbating a couple of times," she said quickly, all in one breath. Darius's eyes were on the floor. "Look, I have absolutely no problem with masturbation. I do it too. In a way, I'm relieved because it's proof that there is still sexual energy in there. I just don't get why he's not sharing that energy with me."

"It's not a big deal, Iman. Sometimes I just need the physical release. It has nothing to do with you." He sat up straight and crossed his arms over his chest, a protective move that told me he was on the verge of shutting down completely.

In our first session, we'd explored the more common reasons for a change in desire. They'd moved in together, he'd changed jobs and was working a lot, Iman had recently gotten off the pill, and pressure to conceive was lurking around the corner. I knew these to be common reasons for a dip in desire, but I also believed Iman—that she was onto something about there being more to the story. She was picking up on something, and honestly, so was I. Darius seemed guarded, quick to play defense against her attempts to get more out of him. As I usually do at this stage in therapy, I scheduled individual sessions with them to see what more I could learn without her there.

Darius returned alone the next week. "Look, I'm not good at this emotional stuff. You've got to remember that I was raised in the Fifth Ward. We didn't exactly talk about our feelings. That would have been a luxury. My mom worked two jobs to keep food on the table. My dad wasn't around, and child support rarely came in. Do you have any idea how many times I got beat up in the neighborhood for being smart? For acting white? The mushy, gushy stuff is a no-go for me. I've really tried with Iman. She's the woman of my dreams, but it's never enough for her."

We explored his upbringing within his family system and his experience being raised in a poor, Black neighborhood. Gifted in math, Darius had been accepted to a prestigious magnet high school in Houston. He earned a full ride to the University of Houston, where he graduated with honors. "I didn't get where I am today by being soft. I'm thankful for the way I was raised. It gave me a backbone and the strength I needed to succeed."

"I hear you," I said, my body feeling heavy after hearing his story, "and I believe you—that your upbringing shaped you in a way that made you successful. But I also wonder who you would be if you'd had the freedom to run down the streets of your neighborhood feeling safe, if you'd had the privilege of having a mom who could be more present with you. I imagine you as a little boy, and I feel many things—I feel sadness, fear, longing." His eyes turned red. "You are successful in many ways. You're thriving by any standard, let alone the context in which you were raised. But Iman wants more from you, not just more sex but better-quality sex. She wants sex that makes you feel connected and bonded as a couple. I'm worried about the long-term success of your marriage if you don't learn how to integrate what you clearly feel emotionally toward her with how you express yourself sexually with her." He was disconnected from an important element of the erotic connection. I wanted to help him find it by helping him tap into his vulnerable side.

In this chapter, we will go to the depths of vulnerability and back again. Vulnerability is at once painful and joyful, and capable of sparking intense pleasure. To quote boxer Muhammad Ali, it can "float like a butterfly, sting like a bee." Our capacity for vulnerability is shaped by our upbringing, and we will explore how our childhoods affect how we understand ourselves, relate to our partners, and express ourselves when making love. Vulnerability is the medium through which we both go deep and play. Let's dive in.

WHAT IS VULNERABILITY?

Vulnerability is powerful. We've historically mischaracterized vulnerability as a weakness, but thanks to important work by vulnerability researcher Brené Brown, we are starting to see that vulnerability may be our greatest strength and an irreplaceable pathway to connection and belonging. When we embrace vulnerability, we believe we are worthy of love and connection despite our mistakes and shortcomings. Brown defines vulnerability as "uncertainty, risk, and emotional exposure."[1] To be vulnerable means you have the courage to put yourself out there emotionally despite the risk that doing so entails. Brown argues, and I wholeheartedly agree, that we cannot have truly intimate relationships without vulnerability.

So how do we get all this from simply making eye contact during sex? Well, eye contact is just a glimmer of how vulnerability can enhance our sex lives. Relationship security, which we'll explore in this chapter, is a prerequisite for vulnerability. It gives us the freedom to be our most complete and authentic selves, which greatly enhances desire and pleasure.

By now, you're familiar with the research study I conducted that examined the role of sensuality and curiosity as it relates to great sex. We know, and this book illustrates, how potent these ingredients are for long-term satisfaction. But there was a catch in the data. The positive correlation between sensuality and curiosity only showed up among individuals in secure relationships. In other words, someone could be the most curious or sensual person in the world, but if they weren't in a relationship that allowed them to feel safe and be vulnerable, it would have little bearing on their sexual pleasure and satisfaction. A key ingredient to a secure relationship is feeling like you can let yourself be seen, that you trust your partner, that you feel safe in your relationship—essentially, vulnerability. Vulnerability is thus arguably the most important element of great sex.

Vulnerability is not just about getting in touch with your emotions. It's about having the curiosity to explore parts of yourself that are hidden or that you've lost touch with so that you can live as a more whole person. We touched on this in the last two chapters, and we will take an even deeper dive here. Vulnerability is also about having the courage to share those parts with your beloved. This chapter will explore how our attachment (i.e., the way we relate to others) inhibits or enhances our ability to be vulnerable. We will discover how practicing self-compassion and healing old wounds helps us access parts of ourselves that are lost or misunderstood. Learning to relate to your partner in a safe and loving way makes it easier (and more fun!) to explore the world and each other. Vulnerability is delicate. This chapter will show you how to discover it in the sweet spot between sharing yourself and practicing healthy boundaries, between pleasure and happiness, and between surrender and control. Together, these components allow us to freely surrender to the bliss that is the human sexual experience.

BARRIERS TO VULNERABILITY

So why is being vulnerable difficult for so many of us? As we'll see in this section, it can stem from unhealthy attachments to others, residual issues from our families of origin, and difficulty setting and maintaining healthy boundaries.

John Bowlby and Mary Ainsworth were the pioneers of what we now refer to as *attachment theory*. Our attachment to others, particularly to our childhood caregivers and our adult romantic partners, can be thought of as the emotional bonds we have with them, and anything that affects our emotional bonds is going to impact our ability to be vulnerable. Attachment can also be thought of as the way we relate to others. We'll explore each attachment style in depth, but for now, consider whether you tend to relate to others with trust and mutual respect or with anxiety and trepidation about possible ulterior motives. Do you find it easy to depend on other people, or are you of the mind that the only person you can depend on is yourself? Bowlby described attachment as a "lasting psychological connectedness between human beings."[2] In other words, our early relationships set the stage for how we relate to others as adults and, in essence, write the blueprint for how vulnerability shows up for us later in life.

As a psychologist, Bowlby reflected on the impact of his own early-childhood relationships. He was only allowed to see his mother for one hour a day after teatime. His father, a respected surgeon, was often absent. He was raised by a series of nannies and describes the feeling of abandonment he had when they left the home. He was sent away to boarding school at age seven. While none of this was necessarily atypical for the time and social class in which Bowlby was raised, as a psychologist, he couldn't help but reflect on how the lack of continuity in these formative relationships impacted him and how different types of parent-child relationships impact others. As a result of his experiences, he became curious about the impact that early-childhood bonds had on psychological development. He drew from many scientific disciplines, including Darwin's work in evolutionary science, and wrote about how our attachment to caregivers had an evolutionary advantage. If we can trust that our adult caregivers respond to and meet our needs, we are more likely to survive in the world. The central tenet of his theory was that if children trust that their caregiver will be available to meet their needs, they will feel safe enough to explore the world around them and go on to thrive in it. This is vulnerability. Think back to Brown's definition: it's about putting yourself out there emotionally despite the risk inherent in doing so. People with unhealthy attachment styles may feel the risk is too great and shut themselves off emotionally as a result. They won't go on to thrive. Let's take a deeper dive into each attachment style to understand the unique impact of each one.

A couple of decades after Bowlby's work, Ainsworth expanded his theory through a series of experiments she called "the strange situation."[3] In these studies, Ainsworth put a toddler and their mother in a new room together. She observed how the child responded when a new person entered the room, how they reacted when the mother left the room, and how they greeted their mother upon her return. Through these interactions, they observed three distinct styles of attachment—secure, anxious, and avoidant.[4] Children who had a secure attachment style would get upset when the caregiver left but were easily soothed when the caregiver returned. They were happy to explore the new environment, periodically checking in with their caregiver to ensure they were still present. Children with an anxious attachment became highly distressed when the caregiver left and were much harder to soothe when the caregiver returned. Furthermore, they tended to be clingy, refusing to explore the environment. These kids were too vulnerable. And finally, children who had an avoidant attachment acted indifferent about the caregiver leaving and indifferent when they returned, some even rejecting the caregiver upon return. These kids were invulnerable. Countless studies have replicated these findings, and we still use these categories to conceptualize the nature of emotional and romantic bonds today.

Later research discovered that these attachment styles tend to replicate themselves in our relationships with our romantic partners as adults.[5] People who have a secure attachment with their romantic partners tend to have strong communication skills and feel confident in their relationships and emotionally close to their partners. They feel that they can freely express their love to their partners and trust that there's an equal give-and-take in the relationship. They feel safe to express their feelings and trust that their partners are emotionally available to them. They are emotionally available to their partners, and they find that the security of the relationship serves as a springboard to feel safe enough to explore the world or take other risks.

One of my research participants, Sarah, described the freedom that her secure attachment gave her. When she married her husband, John, she was thirty-eight and working in HR. She had always dreamed of going back to school to study finance, something John encouraged. At first, this encouragement and support from her partner felt uncomfortable, but it eventually felt wonderful once Sarah leaned in. "I'd kissed my share of frogs before meeting John and initially found it difficult to trust that he'd support me through school," she told me. "As our relationship deepened, however, I found myself relaxing into it in a way I hadn't with other partners. He was so persistent and so reassuring that I finally did it! I graduate next month! I truly believe his support of my dreams is one of the key reasons we have such a passionate sex life."

Alternatively, people who have an anxious attachment style in their relationships tend to be clingy to their partners. They may act possessive or constantly (sometimes subconsciously) come up with little tests to determine whether their partners truly love them. They often believe that they love their partners more than their partners love them. In other words, they are too vulnerable. This was the case with my client Louis. Every time his boyfriend, Mark, traveled for work, Louis would call incessantly. He'd pout if Mark didn't bring him back a gift, accusing Mark of not thinking about him while away. Mark always checked in, but it never seemed to be enough for Louis. Growing tired of never feeling enough for Louis and feeling suffocated by his clinginess, Mark eventually ended the relationship.

Finally, folks who have an avoidant attachment style in their romantic relationships tend to avoid emotional closeness. There is a lack of intimacy. They pride themselves on their independence (which represents their difficulty with vulnerability), and they tend to be dismissive of their partners' feelings. Furthermore, they don't create a space where their partners can freely express their thoughts and feelings. I had started to suspect that Darius's behavior reflected an avoidant attachment style. The way he tuned out Iman during sex and got defensive when she tried to express herself told me that something was going on that made it difficult for him to express the full range of his vulnerability.

We are all born with the propensity for vulnerability, but unfortunately, many of us have early relationships that send the loud and clear message that vulnerability isn't safe. Take Darius—not only did he grow up in a rough neighborhood, which compromised his physical vulnerability, but he also had to meet his own emotional needs since his mom worked so much. The message that vulnerability isn't safe often emerges as a result of physical or emotional abuse or neglect. *Abuse* may be too strong a word for many people—Darius's mom in no way abused him. In these cases, I use the phrase *less-than-nurturing behavior.* Unhealthy or suboptimal parenting can be overt, but it can be subtle too, making it hard to identify and heal from. I've seen countless variations of less-than-nurturing behavior show up among my clients. Yes, they had roofs over their heads and food to eat, but parents failed to nurture them emotionally, which inhibits their ability to be vulnerable in their adult relationships.

My client Anika, for instance, never felt she could talk to her parents when she had a bad day. Rather than giving her space to express her feelings, they'd scold her, dismissing her experience and telling her to toughen up, reminding her constantly that they had it worse growing up. Kai, another client, distinctly remembers the moment he shut down his emotions. He was nine years old and came home with a black eye after a group of boys beat him up on the playground. Rather than teaching him how to handle the conflict or advocating on his behalf to the school administrators, his father looked at him with disgust, rolled his eyes, and walked out of the room. My client Miranda walked on eggshells for most of her childhood. Her mother could be loving and exciting. She remembers trips to the mall and mother-daughter dates at the nail salon, but she also learned to avoid her mother in the evenings after she opened a bottle of wine. The way her mother behaved while tipsy made Miranda feel anxious and uneasy. These examples illustrate how parents created emotional unease in their kids, making it hard for them to fully lean into their vulnerability.

Our attachment styles—anxious, avoidant, or secure—can determine what kind of sex we have. Dr. Sue Johnson, a modern thought leader on the way our attachment styles show up in our adult romantic relationships, found that couples who have an anxious style of attachment have what she calls *solace sex*. These couples use sex to feel reassured in their relationships and experience less physical pleasure as a result. Sex usually leaves them feeling empty since they are relying on it to feel reassured.[6]

People with an avoidant attachment style have what Johnson refers to as *sealed-off sex*. These people maintain emotional distance and use sex primarily to relieve sexual tension or as a way to relish in their sexual prowess. The

bonds with their partners are secondary to the physical release, which usually leaves their partners feeling used, much
like the way Iman felt with Darius.

Finally, people who have a secure attachment style have
what Johnson calls *synchrony sex*. Because of the emotional
closeness and safety in the relationship, these folks feel safe
and vulnerable enough to explore all sides of their eroticism. There's a healthy dose of play and openness, and sex is
an opportunity to feel bonded and loved. Think about how
you feel when you have sex with your partner. Do you feel
like there is a level of synchrony? Do you feel like it is emotionally sealed off? Or do you finish the sexual encounter
only to feel frustrated and dissatisfied because it didn't give
you the reassurance you were seeking in the relationship?

As Johnson says, a secure attachment is what enables one
to let go and enjoy the ride. It's hard to feel safe enough to
reveal your sexual preferences or most private erotic thoughts
with someone you don't trust. One of the ultimate tests of vulnerability in your relationship—or in other words, whether a
partnership is reflective of a secure attachment—is whether
you can look your partner in the eyes when you make love. I
cannot tell you how many times I've given clients this homework exercise only to be met with blank stares. I suspected
Darius would have looked at me the same way had I made
the suggestion to him. I started to think more about how his
upbringing affected emotional vulnerability for him, and
turned to psychotherapist Pia Mellody's model as a frame-
work.

I've always liked Mellody's model of codependency when
thinking about vulnerability and the impact that our early
childhood relationships have on us.[7] Mellody holds that all

children are born with five core attributes—they are all valuable, *vulnerable*, dependent, imperfect, and spontaneous. It's the parents' job to nurture these qualities, within reason. As it relates to vulnerability, it's the parents' responsibility to meet their children's emotional needs in a way that is developmentally appropriate. If Mellody saw the earlier client examples I shared, she'd point out that their parents' inability to create space for the range of their emotional experiences most likely hindered their ability to fully express themselves in a healthy and vulnerable way as adults. Anika wasn't allowed to express "negative" feelings; Kai wasn't allowed to express "weakness"; and Miranda had to tiptoe around her tipsy mother. In each case, the clear message from the parents was, *I cannot accept or tolerate you as a whole and complete person who has a range of emotions.* Darius was no different. Not only had his father abandoned the family, his mom (by no fault of her own) was significantly limited in her ability to spend quality time with him. What free time she had was spent pushing him to succeed in school. Messages like these make us shut down parts of ourselves, which inhibits our ability to show up in the world (and with others) as fully authentic individuals. And when we can't be fully authentic—when we can't express all sides of ourselves—we can't connect with others through vulnerability.

It is important to note that vulnerability does not mean putting everything out there all the time. That would be exhausting and overwhelming. Learning to implement healthy emotional boundaries is an important aspect of vulnerability. In short, a boundary is an imaginary line between you and another person. Boundaries can be physical (e.g., not allowing strangers to touch you) or emotional (e.g., respecting someone's need for space). On one extreme of a healthy boundary is a wall, and on the other extreme is, well, nothing. Healthy boundaries give us the power to express healthy vulnerability *in moderation*. It's not healthy to be *too* vulnerable, nor is it good to be invulnerable.

Children tend to adopt the boundary system modeled by their parents. If parents have weak boundaries, chances are their adult children will too. You may, for instance, push to get your way all the time, completely ignoring others' emotional wants and needs. On the flip side, you could become a doormat, letting others walk all over you. Both extremes represent weak emotional boundaries, which inhibit vulnerability and healthy connection.

Alternatively, when parents have walls instead of boundaries (like Kai's father did), children may learn to close themselves off emotionally. They become walled off and *invulnerable*, making it difficult to connect fully and authentically with others. What do boundaries have to do with great sex? Well, boundaries are, in part, how we understand ourselves in relation to other people. It is not reasonable to expect great sex without great boundaries. In *The Road Less Traveled*, M. Scott Peck asserts, "Ego boundaries must be hardened before they can be softened. An identity must be established before it can be transcended. One must find one's self before one can lose it."[8]

This is why vulnerability is a crucial component to any relationship: the key to softening ourselves is to first know ourselves, and to know ourselves, we must have a strong understanding of our boundaries and attachment patterns in relationships. The good news is that when you have a partner who's willing to work with you, your adult relationship can be a wonderful healing place for wounds that may have been formed early on in your life. Let's explore how to reclaim healthy vulnerability so that we can thrive in the world, in our relationships with others, and between the sheets.

DISCOVERING VULNERABILITY WITHIN YOURSELF

Vulnerability is not just about getting in touch with your emotional side or learning to ask for help; it is about having the courage to explore parts of yourself that you tend to shy away from, that you ignore, or that you've lost touch with. In the last section, I described what factors lead to a breakdown, or compartmentalization, of vulnerability. This section will explore how to reintegrate our internal parts and describe how practicing self-compassion can give us the strength to do so. To do this, we often need to heal our childhood wounds, allowing us to become fully functional adults. Doing so can be scary, but remember—*vulnerability* is an act of courage.

Whether you had childhood trauma or not, whether you had an anxious attachment or a secure attachment, you likely have parts of yourself that are not fully integrated. While some of the jargon may seem antiquated today, I like the way Carl Jung conceptualized the "self," particularly as it relates to masculine and feminine energy.[9] He refers to these two energies as *anima* (the feminine energy present in men) and *animus* (the masculine energy present in women). Anima is receptive, relational, and intuitive. Animus is assertive, logical, and exploratory. If you don't like the loaded gender language here, you can think of these parts as yin and yang. Yin is passive and receptive while yang is active and expansive. Exploring our latent sides offer the opportunity for enormous psychological growth.

I can't tell you how many male clients have longed for their female partners to be more sexually assertive and exploratory (animus) and how many of my female clients long for their male partners to be more tender, intuitive, and to hold them after they make love (anima). This was the side of Darius that Iman yearned for. The more wholly we show up in the bedroom, which can only happen when we feel safe enough to explore our more vulnerable sides and courageous enough to expose our assertive sides, the more exciting and passionate our sexual encounters.

We'll talk about gender socialization more in the next chapter, but for now, I'll say that it is in part responsible for the difficulty we experience in reaching our full psychological potential, particularly as it relates to sex. Entering a sexual encounter too compartmentalized can make the sex feel fractionated. Jung believed that the more fully integrated our masculine and feminine energies were, a phenomenon he refers to as *syzygy*, the more whole we are as individuals. This is not about men becoming more feminine or women becoming more masculine; it's about everybody, no matter where they fall on the gender-identity spectrum, becoming more whole. It takes vulnerability and courage to explore the unknown sides of ourselves.

The Internal Family Systems model of therapy gives us another way of conceptualizing our internal parts. Created by Dr. Richard Schwartz, this model holds that our sense of *Self* is made up of different parts with unique roles.[10] Some parts, called *Exiles*, are parts that our sense of Self tries to eject as a result of pain, shame, or fear—feelings usually caused by childhood trauma. He holds that many people live life with their *Manager* parts at the forefront. Managers attempt to control the way the external world perceives us and try to prevent us from being hurt. In doing so, though, they block us from tapping into our full experience of vulnerability. Darius had an emotionally vulnerable part that his sense of Self had exiled, a phenomenon not uncommon among my male clients.

Trevor Noah, in a between-the-scenes clip of *The Daily Show*, shared his opinion about men's experience of sex and emotional vulnerability. He says,

> [Men complain about how they] aren't "having the sex they want to have," [but] . . . people don't realize how often men are experiencing a lack of intimacy, and the only place they can experience that intimacy is through sex. We've created a society where men are so afraid to be vulnerable with each other . . . to care for each other, to love each other . . . I hope we get to the place where guys go, "Oh, I actually didn't need the sex. I needed to be held, and I live in a society where it's hard to be held unless I'm having sex" . . . And I think if we have a little more of those conversations, a few more honest conversations, a few more vulnerable conversations, we may get to a place where it's not just sex or no sex. It's people saying, "Yeah, we are full human beings who require a full spectrum of affection and affections towards us." And in the same way for many years, great therapists have been saying that women have to be allowed to express that they want and

*enjoy sex, I think we also have to encourage men in society
to go, "I want to express and enjoy intimacy aside and
apart from sex."[11]*

It's hard (especially for men) to be vulnerable enough
to admit that they long for emotional intimacy. Likewise,
women often feel apprehensive when asserting their needs
and desires. It's not uncommon for there to be an inner
voice urging you to just keep quiet. One of the best ways to
quiet the inner critic telling you to avoid vulnerability is to
practice self-compassion.

I vividly remember the day I sat down in Dr. Kristin
Neff's class when I was an undergraduate at the University
of Texas. She had a way of making the class feel immediately
at ease. Everybody loved her. It came as no surprise when
she introduced the concept of self-compassion, which is the
focus of her academic research. I had heard of self-esteem,
but self-compassion was a new concept. I had a sense of
what it meant but didn't fully understand its power until
her class. Being guarded and walled off is the opposite of
vulnerability. It's easy to see how we may be walled off as
it relates to our relationships with others, but the truth is,
we do it to ourselves too. Our guardedness comes in the
form of criticism, pushiness, rigidity, lack of insight, and
defensiveness against no one other than ourselves. We can
be our own worst enemies. When we let down our internal
walls, however, when we become vulnerable with ourselves,
when we move from guardedness to *compassion*, we open
the door to a happier, more meaningful life. In doing so,
we improve the relationships we have with ourselves and,
ultimately, with other people.

In my next session with Darius, I requested his permission to dive deeper. I asked him to close his eyes and picture himself as a little boy coming home from school to an empty house. I watched as his eyes flickered beneath his eyelids, an indication that the memory was vivid. Then I told him to imagine himself as an adult going into the house. "Look at your younger self. Get down on his level. Take his hands into yours, and look at him with loving eyes." Tears silently streamed down his cheeks. "What do you think he needs to hear from you?" I prompted.

"I can't—I can't say it," he stammered.

I helped him out. "You don't have to say this out loud if you don't want to. You can imagine it. But notice how it feels to tell him how much you love him, how proud you are of all his hard work in school, but most importantly—and this is where self-compassion comes into play—give him permission to feel sad about not having a closer relationship with his mother."

I explained to Darius that he could both respect his mother for the difficult choices she made *and* long for more warmth and tenderness from her. I pointed out that his inability to compassionately tap into this more vulnerable side of himself had likely affected his ability to fully express himself with Iman. We worked together to heal and integrate both parts of himself so that he could begin the process of showing up more wholly for Iman.

Inner-child work like this is one of the most powerful ways to heal old wounds that may be preventing you from tapping into your vulnerable side. There are several approaches to inner-child healing that you can try on your own. Consider the following exercise.

Write a Letter to Your Caregiver(s)

This letter is not meant to actually be shared with your caregiver(s). It is for you, and you only.

In this exercise, you will put pen to paper (no typing) and write a letter to your caregiver(s) about how their less-than-nurturing or abusive behavior may have impacted you. I want to reiterate that we can have compassion and understanding for our caregiver(s) while also holding them accountable for their wrongdoings. Inspired by Pia Mellody's work, this exercise is designed to help you identify the gaps in parenting so that you can begin the process of using the skills you have as an adult to heal any inner-child wounds for yourself. Once you write your letter, imagine your caregiver(s) sitting in a chair across the room from you. Then read the letter out loud, imagining that they have no choice but to listen to you. It might go something like this:

Dear _____,
When I was a child, I needed you to (*identify what you needed*). (Examples include: teach me healthy boundaries, model healthy relationships, create space for me to express my feelings, let me play and have fun, give me information about my body and sexuality, etc.)

Instead, you (*identify their abusive / less-than-nurturing behavior*). (Examples include: made it my job to take care of your feelings, hit/spanked me, neglected to offer any sex education, put me in unsafe situations, yelled and screamed at me, held unrealistic expectations of me, etc.)

This left me feeling (*identify the effects of their behaviors*). (Examples include: ashamed, scared, anxious, unable to express myself emotionally, unable to express myself sexually, inhibited in my relationships with others, untrusting of others, overly dependent on others, emotionally avoidant, insecure in my relationships, etc.).

Today, I am reclaiming (*identify what you're reclaiming*). (Examples include: comfort with vulnerability, the courage to connect more intimately with others, autonomy over my sexuality, confidence in myself, etc.)

Thank you for listening.

Exercises like these help heal internal wounds that may prevent us from connecting more holistically with others and fully thriving in the world. Self-compassion gives us an opportunity to judge ourselves positively and relate to ourselves (both our present-day selves and older versions of ourselves) kindly despite the mistakes we make, the suffering we endure, and the failures we experience.

Neff conceptualizes self-compassion as having three core components that work together.[12]

1. Your emotional response to suffering (with kindness or with judgment)
2. How you make sense of your predicament (as part of the human experience or as isolating)
3. How you pay attention to your suffering (with mindfulness or with overidentification—meaning the problem consumes your identity as opposed to being a mere facet of your experience)

When we practice self-compassion, we respond to our pain with mindfulness, kindness, and recognition that it is part of the human experience. This is a process that is echoed in Brené Brown's work on vulnerability as well. She writes about how only through vulnerability and compassion can we connect more completely with others as part of the human experience.

Prior to our work together, Darius was so internally compartmentalized he could hardly identify his pain, let alone practice compassion for it. Thankfully, he had started to soften through his healing work with me. Iman attested to the fact that he seemed more emotionally present and had gotten better about opening up to her about tough days at work. "I'm incredibly thankful for this improvement," she said, "I can feel the change in him emotionally, but things still aren't where I want them to be sexually."

"I'm trying, Iman," Darius said impatiently. "You've got to give me time. Look, I get it now. No one is more disappointed in how I've let you down than I am. In trying to be strong, somehow I haven't been the man you needed. How messed up is that?" Darius couldn't deny the issues any longer, but he was starting to turn to self-critique instead of self-compassion, something I often see as a client begins to redefine their emotional boundaries.

It's not uncommon for people to move between extremes as they are setting healthy emotional boundaries. Darius started to swing from self-compassion to self-critique, which ran the risk of walling him off again. If you're like many of my clients, you probably think you need to criticize yourself to motivate yourself—*Don't be a wuss! You'll never measure up!*—but the research tells a different story. Let's stop for a moment and think about what happens when we criticize ourselves. Neff points out that self-criticism activates the body's fight-or-flight response because we are not just being attacked, we are also the attacker. This taps into the reptilian brain and floods the body with stress hormones like cortisol. Fortunately, we are not reptiles; we are mammals, and mammals' bodies are programmed to respond to warmth, gentle touch, and soft vocal tones. Think of how you'd talk to a child or close friend. Self-compassion helps us stay in the healthy zone of individual vulnerability. Practice self-compassion yourself with the following exercise.

Embracing Self-Compassion

Think of something you tend to criticize yourself about. Perhaps it's your appearance, the way you eat, feelings of relationship or sexual inadequacy, the way you perform at work, a physical limitation, or the kind of parent you are. What shortcoming do you identify?

Now imagine your inner voice as it currently is. What is the tone of your inner voice? What does it sound like? If you imagined this part of you sitting in a chair across from you, what would it look like?

Now soften the inner voice. Imagine that instead of this nagging part, a kind friend, relative, or therapist is sitting in that chair across from you. What would he or she say instead?

How do your thoughts and feelings change when you respond to your perceived inadequacies with loving-kindness? When you remember you're not the only one with this limitation? When you create a mindful, spacious presence with this voice?

How does that change the sensations in your body? How can you position your body or adjust your posture to reflect the kindness you've expressed to yourself?

I reminded Iman to be patient and to give Darius time and space to recalibrate himself as he began the process of re-integration. I reminded them that self-compassion promotes mental well-being, motivation, and responsibility, greater happiness and life satisfaction, and a stronger sense of self-worth and connectedness with others. The fact that Darius and Iman had come this far was major progress. They were making good headway, but their story was far from over.

CREATING VULNERABILITY IN YOUR RELATIONSHIP

We've talked about the honeymoon stage in previous chapters—about how the cocktail of neurochemicals makes sex feel effortless, intense, and spontaneous. But it's also worth exploring how this same intoxicating mix of chemicals can mask issues that may be lurking below the surface. I see this all the time in my practice. Like Darius, people report feeling connected during sex in the early days, but as soon as the honeymoon stage ends, their issues with vulnerability suddenly appear.

Take my client Maria, who couldn't understand how the date rape she experienced in college might have anything to do with the sudden onset of anxiety she felt every time she and her boyfriend Mario made love, a reaction that began eight months into her relationship with her boyfriend. Or my client Tina, a woman with classic avoidant attachment symptoms, whose orgasmic consistency diminished about a year into her relationship with Jeffrey. The more emotionally involved Jeffrey got, the further away she felt herself pull.

In my experience, it's always worth exploring the roles that vulnerability and intimacy play in the onset of sex and relationship issues, especially when those issues begin as the honeymoon stage of the relationship ends. As we'll see in this section, it is not until we heal old wounds that we can tap into the joy of vulnerability in a way that invites playfulness and erotic excitement.

People's issues with attachment, trauma, shame, or other mental health problems abruptly rear their heads as soon as the brain chemistry returns to normal levels. The surge of dopamine during the early days makes for a very intense experience, but true intimacy (which is where vulnerability lives) doesn't come until later in the relationship. People who have issues around intimacy tend to shut down when the intensity isn't there to distract them from what's lurking below the surface. This is why so many people jump from one relationship to another; they are unable to tolerate the vulnerability inherent in healthy intimacy.

There is a period in all relationships when intensity transitions to intimacy. The honeymoon period lasts anywhere between six and eighteen months. During this period of the relationship, you have so much dopamine and other feel-good chemicals surging through your bloodstream, it's as if you're high on cocaine. In this phase of the relationship, everything feels easy and passionate and intense. It's effortless. The problem is that falling in love is a passive process. That's why they call it *falling* in love. Inevitably, the honeymoon period ends, and the rose-colored glasses come off. This has to happen or else we wouldn't get anything done. Inherent in this transition is the conversion of *intensity* into *intimacy*. It was par for the course that Darius's desire began to diminish a year into his relationship with Iman. This is when his avoidant attachment revealed itself and when a self-protective wall snapped up, inhibiting his ability to be vulnerable. Now that I'd done healing work with Darius individually, I wanted to help him open up more emotionally to Iman. While Iman knew how Darius grew up, he hadn't detailed the emotional impact of the experience, or he'd minimized it at best.

I instructed them to sit facing each other on the sofa. "Take each other's hands and see how it feels to hold eye contact," I said.

Darius shifted uncomfortably, but then took a deep breath and settled in. "I feel silly," he said.

"I get it," I responded. "You're not used to communicating this way, but I think there is something powerful about it. Think of how officiants encourage couples to maintain the same posture when exchanging their vows. Looking at each other hand in hand creates intimacy and forces you—in a good way—to be vulnerable."

He nodded in understanding. Iman gave his hands a reassuring squeeze.

"I want you to tap into the courage you have as an adult and use it to bolster the vulnerability that is there below the surface," I continued. "You don't have to be scared of it anymore now that you're in a safe and loving relationship with Iman. I'd like you to see how it feels to open up to her about some of the work we did together on healing your inner child."

Darius took a deep breath and dove right in. He talked to Iman about how lonely he felt growing up, how much he longed for more time with his mother, how scared he felt every time he walked to the bus stop on his way to school.

She'd known him on a surface level, but now understood him in a deeper, more meaningful way. He cried, she cried. Even I teared up, as I usually do in moments like these, when I see powerful intimacy forming right before my eyes. He finally felt courageous enough to explore his inner world.

There are some important distinctions that must be made between the nature of vulnerability in parent-child relationships and that inherent in adult romantic relationships. Vulnerability in adult relationships must happen in moderation. It is not fair to expect your partner to soothe every emotion for you. Adults, to an extent, need to learn how to do that for themselves. Nothing will kill desire faster than being too emotionally needy of your partner. This dynamic starts to mimic the parent-child relationship, which isn't very sexy. I love how the vulnerability movement encouraged openness and sharing, but there is a line. You must make sure there is space for your partner in the relationship too. Healthy vulnerability is not just about your partner being a secure base for you but also you serving as a secure base for your partner. What do you do to encourage your partner to take risks? In what ways do you create space for them to explore? Gauge vulnerability in your own relationship with the following exercise.

Assessing Relationship Vulnerability

Vulnerability can't be forced. It happens over time in the presence of safety and trust. This is an exercise in building emotional safety and trust in your relationship. You'll apply what you've learned about self-compassion to this exercise to create an environment of comfort both for yourself and for your partner.

In this exercise, you'll prepare a foundation of safety in preparation to be vulnerable with your partner.

You Try It:

Spend some time reflecting on whether or not you currently cultivate a safe space for your partner to open up about their feelings. Now that you've practiced self-compassion, you should be able to be honest, yet gentle with yourself. What do you do that might foster an environment of openness? What do you do that might create an environment that makes your partner shut down?

How do you respond when your partner shares a concern, fear, or hope?

To what degree do you ask questions to fully understand your partner's feelings? To what degree do you dismiss your partner's feelings or experiences as being unimportant?

Healthy vulnerability doesn't mean sharing every little thought and feeling that comes to mind, and it certainly doesn't mean expecting your partner to pacify every anxiety that comes up for you. Inherent in the transition from childhood to adulthood is the learned skill of doing this for yourself. Vulnerability, which can happen internally as well as interpersonally, is also about knowing when to self-soothe, especially if your partner needs some breathing room.

David Schnarch, in his book *Passionate Marriage*, refers to this as *differentiation* (a concept originally coined by psychologist Murray Bowen).[13] In essence, differentiation is about having the ability to stand on your own two feet *while at the same time* maintaining a connection to your partner. A major component of differentiation is learning how to regulate your own emotions so that you don't over-rely on your partner to do so for you. (Cue self-compassion tools from earlier.) It's about knowing where you end and your partner begins.

I checked in with Darius and Iman a few weeks later. They looked radiant. "Tell me how things have been going," I prompted eagerly.

"Amazing!" Iman declared. "I feel more connected to him than ever before. We finally made love without breaking eye contact. It was so powerful, I cried afterward. Not sad tears, of course; they were happy tears. Tears of relief and of overwhelming love. Tears of finally feeling seen after so many years of being shut out. I was worried my emotion would make Darius pull back, but it didn't. He held me gently and stroked my back until we both fell asleep. It was bliss."

It is with these skills—vulnerability in moderation and healthy differentiation—that we can discover the intensity that is present within intimacy. Do you remember how I said that a lot of people jump ship when intensity transitions to intimacy because they think the passion is gone? Think again. Consider the proverb "Shallow brooks are noisy, but still waters run deep." In *The Road Less Traveled*, Peck points out that "in the muted, controlled hues of a Rembrandt one can find the color, yet infinitely more richness, uniqueness, and meaning. Passion is a feeling of great depth."[14]

I talked to Darius and Iman about how they felt about their therapeutic progress. "Do you feel like you're ready to end our work together?" I asked.

They looked at each other and then at me.

Darius jumped in. "We are thrilled with where we are now, but as much as we love this newfound emotional connection . . ." He paused. "It would be nice to mix in some playfulness too. I want to make love, but I want to have some fun too."

I smiled and laughed. "You bring up such a great point!" I told them. "Absolutely—let's talk about that. What you have right now is a solid foundation. You're healing your attachment and vulnerability issues in and through your relationship with Iman, which will give you everything you need to explore your more playful side. Remember—it's only when we are courageous enough, which we get through healthy vulnerability, that we can feel confident enough to explore." It was exciting to see this side of Darius emerging, and I sensed it was refreshing for Iman.

"He's gotten so serious with this new job," she said. "As much as I wanted to be seen by him again, I also want to regain our sense of lightheartedness. We used to have fun together."

"I completely agree," I told them. "Let's get that back too."

One of the best benefits of a secure attachment and relationship vulnerability is that it gives you the freedom to play. Your partner is your playmate in the game of life. You may as well have fun with them. As Plato once said, "You can discover more about a person in an hour of play than in a year of conversation."

When I think of adults and play, one of the first things that comes to mind is the episode of *Friends* titled "The One Where Phoebe Runs." Phoebe and Rachel decide to go running in Central Park, but much to Rachel's chagrin, Phoebe starts running like a wild child, arms and legs flailing everywhere. Phoebe insists that running like this is more fun, but Rachel, too embarrassed to be seen with her, creates excuses to run alone. Eventually, Rachel, feeling bored on one of her solo runs, decides to try Phoebe's style and runs straight into her friend, who could not be more delighted. "You're right!" Rachel exclaims. "I feel so free!" Playfulness is a key ingredient to relationship and sexual happiness because it helps us feel free even within the confines of daily life.

For many of us, our lightheartedness and sense of play and adventure go out the window as we mature. By now, you know that we are made up of many internal parts. Everyone, somewhere deep inside, has a part that likes to play and have fun. While constant silliness can sometimes serve as a mask to more vulnerable parts, it's incredible when it happens as part of the full range of human emotion. It's hard to lean into your playful part if you're not comfortable with vulnerability. Playfulness helps keep the mood light and creates a sense of ease with your partner. If one person is having a great time during play, it's hard not to have a good time too. This energy within the relationship carries over into the bedroom. Try to think about the last time you and your partner shared a good belly laugh about something. When was the last time you chased each other around outside?

Many large organizations have acknowledged the importance of play. Companies like Google and Apple have entire "playrooms" in their corporate offices. These are available for employees to use throughout the day. These playrooms are replete with foosball tables, pinball machines, and bag-toss games. CEOs have discovered that giving their employees a chance to relax, let go, and reconnect with play-induced creative energy has massive benefits to work performance.[15] When stuck in front of a computer screen or boardroom all day long, employees' perspectives start to narrow. They get stuck on their individual ideas as opposed to engaging in creative brainstorming as a group. As we discussed in the previous two chapters, this kind of narrow-minded thinking is the antithesis of flexibility and openness.

If play is a critical ingredient for childhood development and corporate growth, why shouldn't it also be an essential component for relationships?[16] Research tells us that it most certainly should. We have plenty of evidence to suggest that play has the same benefits for adults—not just for us as individuals but in our romantic relationships too. Couples who play together stay together. Studies consistently find that play helps maintain happiness, trust, and strong connections for the long haul.[17]

One exercise I love to give my clients is to go to a nearby children's park and just swing. I instruct them to notice the feel of the wind in their hair, the thrill of the swing going higher and higher as they pump their legs. "If you dare," I tell them, "leap off at the peak of the swing. See how it feels to do something you once loved as a kid."

Think back to the early days of your relationship. Chances are you went to great lengths to have fun together and keep the mood light. We lose sight of how important that is when we get bogged down with things like bills, long commutes, and kids. Kids, by the way, run the risk of zapping us of all our playful energy. Note to parents—make sure you reserve some of that energy for your partner too. Studies show that playfulness in romantic relationships promotes intimacy, reduces conflict and tension, and enhances communication.[18] Having playful day-to-day interactions, nicknames for each other, and gentle teasing deepens bonds, facilitates communication, and helps couples learn conflict-resolution strategies. Think about what you learn about someone from how they respond to losing a game. Someone who plays a lot gets better at losing and is more likely to take conflict in stride compared to someone who has less experience.

In a 2021 blog post, play researcher Carol Bruess points out that "[playful rituals] are profound ways of nourishing our relationships, infusing them with shared joy and sensibilities. What's more, research on laughter and humor reveals that when we laugh, our fears are disarmed a bit. We are more willing and open to hearing others' opinions, even if they are ones with which we strongly disagree. We feel heightened vitality in our bonds. Anger is more quickly re-leased. And laughter helps us forgive others more quickly."[19]

It was time to explore the ways in which Darius and Iman envisioned playfulness reentering their relationship. Iman had mentioned that she had walked in on Darius masturbating a couple of times. I was curious to learn more about what turned him on. I suspected, given the fact that he'd shut down so much with Iman, he hadn't let her in on his inner sexual world. After I spoke with him individually, he felt ready to share some of his turn-ons with Iman. Sharing the intricacies of your unique sexuality is perhaps one of the most courageous acts of vulnerability. Our sexuality is so personal that putting it out there for someone else to potentially judge or reject can feel extremely intimidating.

I reminded them how important it is to create an environment of safety and trust. Opening up about our sexuality takes guts. Fear of rejection is hardwired into our DNA. Hundreds of thousands of years ago, being rejected from the social group meant certain death (no one could survive without the group), so it's no wonder putting ourselves out there at risk of rejection activates the nervous system. I reminded Iman that no matter what Darius shared—even if it was something that turned her off or surprised her—that it would be best to respond with neutrality and curiosity. If it wasn't something she liked, she had every right to let him know as long as she communicated with respect, kindness, and compassion.

Darius started. "I kind of have a teacher-student thing."

Iman's eyes widened, but she held her composure and took a deep breath. "What do you mean?" she asked. "In what way?"

"Like, I get turned on by the idea of being seduced by

a teacher figure. It's not the only thing that turns me on, of course, but it is something I search for when I'm on the internet."

I jumped in and explained that after exploring this fantasy with Darius in one of our individual sessions together, we'd determined that this could have developed as a response to his own upbringing. He more or less had to figure out life on his own. As a result, he'd eroticized the idea of an older, more experienced woman showing him the ropes. Sometimes a fantasy has absolutely no connection to our pasts, but other times it does. Sex can give us the opportunity to feel a sense of control over something we may not have had control over in the past.

Darius picked up again. "I thought it could be kind of fun if we, um, role-played this scenario sometime."

Iman smiled. "I think I could get behind that idea."

If only all my clients were so receptive!

There is perhaps no better space for couples to play than in the bedroom. Play helps deepen emotional bonds, and as we'll see, stronger bonds facilitate play.

CULTIVATING VULNERABILITY IN EROTICISM

Our ability to connect emotionally during sex is one of the key components that makes us different from animals. Sex is so much more than a union of physical bodies. When we share our bodies with another person, we are bringing everything we have been, everything we are, and everything that we hope to be into that moment. If we feel like we're in a relationship in which we can't bring parts of ourselves into the bedroom, then we're not bringing all our humanness into the erotic encounter. Sex, if you pay attention, feels empty when the emotional connection isn't there. In this final section on vulnerability, we will explore the different ways our attachment styles manifest themselves in the erotic realm, the benefits of emotion-driven (as opposed to hormone-driven) sex, and how to strike vulnerability in the balance of pleasure and enjoyment.

Sex and relationship research tells us that emotional closeness goes hand in hand with sexual satisfaction.[20] The health of your relationship and the degree of emotional intimacy (i.e., vulnerability) you feel in your partnership correlates strongly to sexual pleasure and satisfaction.

My client Pamela, a business consultant, was a good example of what happens to sexual satisfaction when emotional closeness is removed from the equation. She didn't understand why her longtime boyfriend didn't feel satisfied with the fact that she was up for anything. She let him tie her up, she wasn't afraid of anal, but he kept pestering her about wanting sex that was more intimate, which she assumed meant "boring" vanilla. She thought of herself as every man's dream girlfriend but didn't realize that her inability to be vulnerable was putting her relationship at risk. She looked at me with utter confusion when I brought up the idea of making love with her eyes open. It took several sessions to help her understand that slow, intimate, eyes-open sex could be just as, if not more, erotic.

She wasn't the first client to have this reaction. I bring up this exercise and visibly see my clients shrink. It's often an early indicator for me that there's not enough safety and emotional closeness in their relationship that would allow them to be mutually transported to such a sacred space. It's quite incredible actually. Making love with your eyes open can be so powerfully intense that it opens your heart, allowing your body to move in rhythm with the flow of emotional energy. If we've talked about the body (sensuality) and the mind (curiosity), this part is the heart.

One of my research participants, Isla, illustrated this when she told me about how her husband opened his heart up to her again after returning from Iraq. Mark had been deployed for two years and was emotionally shut down for a long time after his return. She made it clear he could talk to her but never pushed for information. She said that one night, he told her that he'd been thinking a lot about his time there and began to sob and sob. And sob. He didn't share details with her, but he released a lot of emotion, and she was there to hold him when he did. She hardly had the words to describe the intensity of their lovemaking after he finally opened up with her. Her ability to create safety and security for him helped him be vulnerable and reconnect with her in a profound and meaningful way.

You want to do everything you can to foster an environment of trust and safety in your relationship. Your sex life will thank you. Put your skills to the test with the following exercise.

Expanding Your Sexual Comfort Zone

It's time to try something new! This exercise should be fun. Reflect back on your Sexual Likes and Dislikes exercise and identify something you haven't tried before. This may be something as simple as making out in the laundry room, or it may be something a bit more adventurous like experimenting with role-play or bondage.

By now, you should feel safe enough to let go and bring a sense of playfulness into your erotic encounter. At the end of the day, this may or may not become a part of your usual sexual repertoire. The only goal of this should be to have fun and create a new experience together.

You Try It:

Discuss and make any preparations ahead of time. Share any concerns, hopes, or other feelings you might have. When you feel ready, go ahead and experiment. Discuss the outcome and answer the following questions.

1. How did you feel before, during, and after the encounter?

2. What shift, if any, did you notice in your relationship leading up to the encounter?

3. What did you notice in the days following this encounter—about yourself and about your relationship?

I checked in with Darius and Iman after they experimented with his role-play fantasy. "How did things go?" I asked.

"It was interesting," Iman started, a look of hesitation on her face. "I felt super awkward."

Darius jumped in. "I thought it was incredible."

Iman smiled at him.

"Tell me more," I prompted. "How specific were you about what you had in mind, Darius?"

"I told her I wanted to play innocent and let her show me the ropes. We pretended that I visited her during office hours and had to do what she said if I wanted to get an A in the class."

I looked at Iman with a raised eyebrow, prompting her to share what the experience was like for her.

"I'm not going to say that I was turned off by the whole thing," she said. "It felt good to see him so excited and to know that I was playing a part in helping him explore his fantasy. Does it turn me on as much as it does him? No. But I love him, and I'm happy to do it every now and then. I'm sure with practice, I'll be able to get into it a bit more. And I know that he's willing to do things that I enjoy too. There is plenty that we both love, so I'm willing to step outside my comfort zone on occasion for him."

"I love what I'm hearing," I told them. "The fact that you are both willing to stretch for each other and that you feel safe enough to expose your desires is the most important thing."

When you feel safe enough to own your sexual desires and put them out there for your partner to share, you'll enjoy a sexual relationship in which there are no barriers. As we can see from the explanation of attachment, humans have two fundamental needs—the need for stability and security along with the need for adventure and novelty. Allowing yourself to *surrender* to other emotions—naughtiness, playfulness, seduction, you name it—is an exercise in personal and relationship vulnerability as well as a key to maintaining passion and spark.

Dr. Peggy Kleinplatz, a sex researcher who studies couples who have magnificent sex, identified *vulnerability and surrender* as a key component of optimal sex. Before I detail her findings, I want to take a closer look at that word *surrender*. An inability to let go, or surrender, is something that many of my clients struggle with. Many cite it as the culprit of their orgasmic difficulties or the reason for their inability to fully immerse themselves in the sexual experience. If you're one of those people, keep reading, because I'm about to rock your world.

Vulnerability paves the way to experiencing one of Mihaly Csikszentmihalyi's most interesting components of flow—control. Many of us hear the word *control* and think of it as the opposite of surrender. It's not. Control, as it relates to flow, is more about the *illusion* of control versus real control. I had to spend time reflecting on the concept of control as it relates to sex. At first, it seemed like a component that didn't fit my thesis. Pick up just about any book on sexuality, and you see the word *surrender* more than anything else, a concept that at first glance seems to be on the opposite side of the spectrum. The more I thought about it, however, the more I realized that control and surrender are not mutually exclusive. In fact, *surrender is not possible if you're not also in control.* As I reflected on my own experiences and read through transcripts of the interviews I had with people who had great sex, I realized that both could be experienced at the same time. Control and surrender, it turns out, are completely different phenomena and, to a degree, dependent on each other. Vulnerability, as we'll see, lies in the balance between the two.

Consider the following example of control as it relates to surrender. I love snow skiing. I try to get on the mountain once a year if I can. I spend the first day warming up on greens, gradually working my way up to blues. By the second or third day, I try to challenge myself on a black, but it's usually a one-and-done. The challenge is just too far above my skill set (remember this concept from chapter 2, "The Excitement of Curiosity"?) for me to enjoy myself. Blues are perfect for me because they beautifully hit that challenge/skills ratio. *I feel in control, which allows me to surrender to the experience.* I set my speed such that my body relaxes, and the rest of the world disappears. My worries completely vanish as I fly down the mountain. It's just me and the sound of my skis cutting the snow, the cold air whipping my face. Even as I write this, I can connect with the feeling in my body. I'm focused and present. I'm fully embodied. All the flow elements are there.

One year, we invited some friends to ski with us. My friends, who grew up in Switzerland, are excellent skiers— far better than I am. One of the friends, who'd worked as a ski instructor two decades prior, made it his mission to get me confidently down a black. His encouragement plus the desire to keep up with the group was all I needed to bite the bullet. He watched me ski some blues and gave me pointers that made a huge difference in my skiing. Once I felt good about having incorporated the changes to my technique, I was ready to tackle a black.

I stood at the top of the slope and watched my friends zip down the mountain. The friend who was coaching me skied down about a hundred yards and waited patiently for me to take off, ready to give me pointers as needed to make it down the rest of the mountain. Trusting my new skills, I pushed off with more power than I usually do at the top of a black. The problem was, I did not feel in control whatsoever. I felt my heart lurch into my chest, certain I was going to crash and burn. Rather than feeling present in my body, I felt disembodied. It felt like the mountain was closing in around me. I lost my balance, my poles flying out in a desperate attempt to regain control, which thankfully I did. *That momentary loss of control made surrender impossible.* I took my time traversing the mountain, slowly skiing at a ninety-five-degree angle, which helped me slow down until I made it down to my friend.

"I'm terrified," I told him. "I don't think I can make it down the mountain."

"Take a deep breath. Look out on the horizon. Have you ever seen anything so beautiful?" he asked.

I looked out. That momentary experience of awe (remember Lani Shiota's research from chapter 1, "The Indulgence of Sensuality"?) helped me relax and return to my body.

"You've got this," he said. He explained what I had done wrong and gave me one last look of encouragement before skiing down another hundred yards. He gave me a thumbs-up. I pushed off, much slower this time. I stayed in control, but I was too in control this time. I was too tense to let go and surrender to the experience the way I could on blues. I was too far in my head, calculating the angle of my skis and the tilt of my body as I cut across the mountain.

I eventually made it down the slope and took on a few more blacks before ultimately deciding to stick to blues for the rest of the day. I wanted to return to the feeling of surrender and freedom that blues give me. I may try again next year, but chances are, you'll find me on the blues.

Csikszentmihalyi describes control as lacking "the sense of worry about losing control that is typical in many situations of normal life."[21] When someone experiences a sense of control during flow, it is the *possibility* of control rather than the *actuality* of control. Vulnerability is about being comfortable with the possibility of control as opposed to the actuality of control. Even though I feel in control on a blue, I'm not in as much control as I think. Skiing is a notoriously dangerous sport. I could hit a patch of ice. I could miscalculate the incline and cut too sharply, obliterating my ACL. Another skier could lose control and plow into me at thirty miles per hour. But . . . I have a sense of control, even in this risky pastime, which allows me to blissfully surrender to the mountain. Being in a relationship with someone who makes us feel safe, who creates space for us to be vulnerable and open, gives us this same feeling of control, which makes it easier to surrender during sex.

Do you remember in the previous chapter how Viktor Frankl and Eranda Jayawickreme described being in control of one's responses rather than to the environment itself? That's a good way to think about the control I'm describing here. Having trust in oneself, practicing self-compassion, and connecting with a supportive partner are all you need to both stay in control and surrender to the experience.

This theme came up among several of my own research participants. James, for example, did a good job describing his experience of control and surrender during sex. "When my wife and I make love and it happens at that really optimal level, everything clicks. I feel completely in control of the situation, but not in the sense I'm controlling her or even myself. It's not about that, because I also let go. There is a sense of effortlessness, like when you're falling, but also the feeling that I have the safety net of a parachute. It's a paradox because while I feel 'in control,' I also experience total surrender to her and to the love I feel for her."

Another research participant, Theresa, illustrated the relationship between control and surrender in her sexual experiences. "I think back to the sex I had in my younger years. I thought I was surrendering in those days, but I wasn't—at least not like I do now. Yes, it was exciting because it was all new, and that was thrilling. But I had no idea what I was doing. I didn't climax regularly, because I didn't have the confidence to ask for what I wanted in bed. I can't tell you how many times I faked my own orgasm for the sake of my partner's ego. My enthusiasm for the encounter depended on theirs. As painful as it was to go through a divorce in midlife, I'm so thankful for it. I'm far more confident in my late forties than I was in my twenties. This confidence gives me a greater sense of agency and control in my sexual encounters. I have partners now who work with me to maximize pleasure. Surrender deepens as I remain confident in my ability to control my own pleasure. Does that make sense? As we establish more trust and safety with each other, as we learn each other's bodies, we both feel more in control, which makes it easier to let go."

Now that my control freaks can take a deep breath, let's go back to what Kleinplatz said about vulnerability and surrender. She writes:

> *Extraordinary lovers argued with their partners at times about sex and other matters, but they trusted each other enough to stay present even when they were uncomfortable, thus expanding their individual and shared comfort zones. They chose to communicate about their desires, even when they differed, with precision and transparency. In the face of struggles in their relationships, they chose to remain emotionally available even when that was scary, in the hope that the resulting vulnerability would be cherished as a gift.*[22]

What Kleinplatz describes here is what happens in intimate, mature relationships. This kind of erotic communication is unlikely to happen in the early stages of the relationship. Honeymoon stage sex is more driven by neurochemicals (not to say it's devoid of emotion, but it lacks mature intimacy). Sex further down the line of a relationship is more emotion-driven, which gives it that more meaningful, transcendent feeling.

In the early stages of a new relationship, we are flooded with dopamine, and serotonin levels dip.[23] Dopamine is a key player in the reward system of the brain. It's the chemical that says, *That was amazing, give me more of that.* Interestingly, the dip in serotonin may explain why we obsess about new partners; serotonin is low in people who have obsessive-compulsive disorder. Eventually, though, as the initial intensity wears off, dopamine levels subside, and serotonin returns to normal. I believe it is this neurochemical transition that makes people think sex is no longer pleasurable in the passion-driven sense.

Since we are discussing neurochemicals, it's worth outlining the neurochemical cocktail produced when we are in flow. In addition to dopamine (the reward chemical), oxytocin (the cuddle hormone), and serotonin (the calming, peaceful neurochemical), we also get a hit of norepinephrine, which boosts energy and alertness. And if that's not enough, our system also floods with endorphins and anandamide, both potent painkillers and stress relievers.[24] Since we know serotonin dips during the honeymoon stage of a relationship, we can argue that experiencing flow during sex in the later stages of a relationship (when serotonin is rebalanced) is what gives us the ultimate high.

It is worth exploring the difference between pleasure and happiness because you need both for long-term erotic passion. Vulnerability lies in the balance between pleasure and happiness. Dr. Robert Lustig summarizes the key differences between pleasure and happiness. Pleasure, he says, is driven by dopamine while happiness is driven by serotonin.[25] He asserts that pleasure is short-lived, while happiness is long term. Pleasure is visceral (meaning you feel it in your body); happiness is ethereal (meaning you feel it in heart and soul). This ethereal feeling is that extra element I'm describing in this chapter. Sex with casual partners can be lots of fun and incredibly pleasurable, but a lot of people find that over time, the pleasure feels empty. I think that's because the dopamine isn't balanced by the serotonin that comes from meaningful relationships and connection. I am not at all opposed to no-strings-attached sex, but I think it's important to think about how emotion can add a vibrant and complex layer to the physical act that leads to greater feelings of sexual fulfillment in the long term.

Csikszentmihalyi similarly differentiates between pleasure and enjoyment. Both Lustig and Csikszentmihalyi argue that we need pleasure. Without it, we wouldn't have the will to live. But pleasure alone, Csikszentmihalyi points out, does not lead to psychological growth. It does not add to complexity of the self.

With Iman's support, Darius had finally leaned into his own complexity. In doing so, they deepened their relationship and reinvigorated their sex life. I check in with them from time to time and can report that our work together was only the beginning of what turned out to be a rich, exciting, and passion-filled emotional and sexual life together.

Vulnerability is a potent and vibrant ingredient of long-term passion. It is rich with nuance in the sense that our ability to be vulnerable as adults is informed by the way we were loved growing up. It is something that can grow and evolve, much like a living, breathing organism, when tended to with loving care. Its delicate balance lies between pleasure and happiness, between control and surrender, and between sharing ourselves and containment. Vulnerability, as we've now learned, paves the way for full and complete authentic self-expression, relational intimacy, and erotic depth.

5

THE EXHILARATION OF ATTUNEMENT

Sharing different heartbeats in one night.
"Heartbeats" by The Knife

G rowing up, I loved to dance—ballet, modern, tap, jazz. You could usually find me in a leotard and tights. I spent countless hours practicing, twirling, leaping, and pirouetting. I enjoyed the discipline of ballet, the freedom of modern dance, the lightheartedness of tap, and the joy of jazz. For me, dance was more than an excuse to dress up in glittery costumes. The training could be rigorous and painful at times. I remember tending to blistered toes and icing twisted ankles. I often had to scarf down fast food in the car on the way to practice and stay up extra late doing homework to accommodate the hours spent in the dance studio each evening. But it was worth it. It was worth it because, for me, dance was an escape. No matter what I had going on at school or home, dance had a way of making my problems disappear. Often, a ninety-minute dance class felt like a half hour. I would become so absorbed in the movement that the pain of my aching feet would subside to the extent that my pointe shoes felt like extensions of my own feet.

As much as I loved dance, it eventually became apparent that I would not go on to be a principal ballerina in a top dance company. I was good, but my ability had begun to plateau. Plus, as I got further into high school, my interests widened. I didn't want to miss out on social events. Academics were important to me too. I didn't want my endless hours of dance to interfere with my grades and social life. So, with sadness and reluctance, I gave it up.

Through college and graduate school, I felt the absence of that "thing" in my life that made everything else disappear. I noticed an uptick in my anxiety. I knew I needed to find a way to get back into dancing.

I decided to try something new. I felt more connected to my Cuban roots than ever before after my trip back to the island and wanted to find ways to express that side of myself back home. So, finally, in my midtwenties, I decided to give salsa dancing a try.

Many of the Latin restaurants in Houston, where I live, have a live-music night, and I had heard that some of them offered free salsa dancing lessons before the band started. I was a little apprehensive, so I convinced a few friends to come along with me to a spot called Gloria's. We had dinner, and as we sipped our margaritas, the restaurant staff began to clear out the tables to make space for the dance floor. Soon, an instructor came forward and invited us to follow along as he demonstrated the basic steps. I needed a little warming up but was relieved to find that those ballet classes years ago had proved useful. I picked up the basics quickly and was excited about what else I could learn.

As it got close to the time for the band to start, the skilled dancers began to make their way into the restaurant. My beginner friends and I could feel the eyes of the experienced dancers sizing us up as they casually sipped their cocktails. I became a little self-conscious as the musicians got ready to play, but even this served to heighten the excitement, and I was eager to see where the night and the music would take me.

When the band started, my friends and I got up to dance. We didn't really know what we were doing yet, but we kept a positive attitude and enjoyed the opportunity to have fun together. With every song, we improved, laughing through our missteps. We could see a few of the advanced dancers moving around us as they made their way onto the dance floor. They were all excellent, and for a moment, I felt just the slightest hint of intimidation. Just then, one approached our group. I began to move away when, to my surprise, he asked me if I wanted to dance. I warned him that I was a beginner, but he winked and told me not to worry about it.

We hit it off immediately. It felt as if "the universe" had sent me the exact mentor I needed in that moment. Miguel was incredibly patient, stopping during the song to help me get back on beat, explaining how I should turn when he lifted my hand a certain way. It wasn't just what he said or did, it was his way of being. He was easygoing, kind, and understanding. He didn't make me feel like he was trying to show off. It was quite the opposite, in fact. He had once been a novice himself, and I could see he enjoyed sharing all that he'd learned over the years. His modest attitude made it a pleasure to learn from him. We danced together for several songs, and I began to feel more confident. By the end of the night, I knew I would be back.

I also knew that if I really wanted to excel, I would have

to take some formal classes. I went to classes once a week and went out social dancing as much as I could. I realized that the same group of dancers showed up each week at the restaurant, so I had the opportunity to dance with Miguel regularly. Over time, I evolved into one of the more experienced dancers myself, filing in right before the band started. Salsa gave me the escape I was craving from my hectic schedule, which included long hours at the office as I was building my new therapy practice. Dancing didn't lessen my workload but rather allowed me to escape it for a while and return feeling more refreshed. With time, practice, patience, and a regular partner, I was able to once again lose myself in the experience, much as I had with ballet ten years earlier. I remember nights when I would spend so much time on the dance floor, I would go home with my hair slicked down with sweat, literally peeling off my jeans before collapsing into bed. My feet ached—this time from dancing in high heels rather than on my toes—but I didn't care. Dance once again gave me the outlet I needed.

These days, I don't make it out to Gloria's as often, but when I do, if I run into Miguel, we always dance one song. It brings back the feelings of discovery and enjoyment that I experienced that first night. What started out as a learning session eventually evolved into a completely fluid and enjoyable collaboration between two friends. My partner and I became so attuned to each other that we were able to simply let go and dance. We became so used to dancing together that I could totally lose myself in the experience—quieting my analytical mind, letting go of the distractions and stresses of my day, and allowing my body and emotions to take over. There are other experienced dancers I partner up with, of course. I have fun when I dance with them, but I don't lose myself the way I do with Miguel, because I don't have as much experience dancing with them. Their footwork may be different; they may dance LA style versus Cuban salsa; they may be much taller, making the turns feel a little awkward, but with Miguel, without conscious thought, I know what the subtlest shift in his weight, flick of his wrist, or shift in his eye contact is signaling my body to do. The experience feels simultaneously meditative and dynamic, where my energy is focused yet free. This was only possible because my dance partner and I were able to reach a state of *attunement*, which is the final secret to reaching flow in your life—and, for the purposes of this book, in your sex life.

This chapter will tie together everything we've learned so far. Now that you understand how to get in touch with your body and open your mind and heart, you'll learn how to put everything together to change your behavior in a way that will lead to *transcendent* sex. I'll explain how emotional intelligence leads to relationship intelligence, which leads to erotic intelligence. This is where all the elements of flow collide, creating a glittering cascade of fireworks. This kind of sex leaves you feeling like time seems to speed up or slow down. It makes you forget who you are while at the same time deepening your understanding of yourself. It makes you feel at one with your partner and with the experience as a whole. Sound too good to be true? The finish line is in sight. This chapter is your final push.

WHAT IS ATTUNEMENT?

All the concepts and theories explained in this book thus far have been leading to the most important secret: attunement. Attunement is the hardest concept to define, but that is what makes it so special. Attunement can be thought of as the magical resonance or sense of harmony we feel when being in sync with another person. It gives us the feeling of bliss, transcendence, effortlessness, and magic. It gives us a deep sense of individual being, of interpersonal belonging and erotic rapture.

As humans, we are hardwired for attunement. Deep within our brains are unique cells called *mirror neurons*. When we see another person doing something like enjoying a warm chocolate chip cookie, these cells can make us feel as if we ourselves are enjoying that same cookie. The effect is so intense that when brain scans are conducted on the "cookie observers," if you will, the areas in their brains involved in taste, smell, and pleasure light up almost as much as if they were the ones who had just savored a bite.[1]

Our brains do this naturally and automatically in many scenarios, but many people struggle to experience the mirroring effect during sex. The reasons vary, but usually have to do with many of the barriers we've discussed in this book and will continue to explore in this chapter—inability to stay present in their bodies, anxiety, the negative effects of culture and socialization, and a culture that increasingly focuses on meeting one's individual needs (i.e., "me culture") as opposed to the group's needs. Rather than tuning in to each other and feeling in sync, many of my clients find that they fumble through sex, practically forgetting that one of the most enjoyable components is the *mutual, synergistic* experience of pleasure. It can feel frustrating to have sex with someone who doesn't seem responsive to, let alone in tune with, your physical and emotional cues, especially when you've been together for a while.

Sloane and Cameron, a couple in their midfifties, came to see me for help getting more sexually in sync. They had done plenty of talking about sexual likes and dislikes but felt that it was making things worse rather than better.

"I'm not sure how to explain the issue," Cameron began, "but sex feels awkward. Kissing is great, so I don't understand where we are going wrong."

"I agree," said Sloane. "We've been together for twenty years. I've always worried that maybe we weren't sexually compatible, but we were so distracted by work that we didn't let it worry us too much. Besides, we always enjoyed kissing each other, and isn't that supposed to be a good sign of sexual chemistry? We're at a point in our lives now where the sexual issue has moved to the forefront of our consciousness. We don't want to split up, but neither of us wants to go the rest of our lives feeling sexually stuck. This is our last hope."

I gathered some history and learned that Sloane was a partner at a top law firm and Cameron was an engineer at NASA. They never had children because they were so focused on their careers. This wasn't a regret. They were both passionate about their work and enjoyed the fruits of their labor. But they had reached a point where they were no longer climbing the career ladder. Life had stabilized, which forced them to pay closer attention to their emotional and sexual relationship. The lack of synchrony they felt wasn't just present in sex. Now that they had more time on their hands, they were bickering more too. Was their relationship at a stalemate, or was there still hope of finding a deeper connection?

This sort of sexual mis-attunement, if you will, was something I'd heard several clients complain about over the years. I've had clients express frustration that their partner seems to do what they see in porn as opposed to what feels good to them as a unique individual. Others use words like *robotic* or *awkward* to describe the sex they have. Some lament that their partners don't seem at all receptive to their sexual feedback; that their requests seem to go in one ear and out the other. The feeling of being "off" happens in relationships too. I've treated couples who have cycled through countless therapists, all offering more or less the same communication exercises, only to find that they still feel out of sync.

So, why is it that so many people feel like their (or their partners') ability to sense and respond to them disappears during sex? Surely our mirror neurons don't simply shut down when we make love. Let's explore some of the more common barriers to attunement.

BARRIERS TO ATTUNEMENT

Many of the barriers we explored in the previous chapters have the propensity to inhibit attunement as well. Our high-tech and fast-paced world, the influence of culture and gender socialization, and our family of origin and trauma all affect our ability to attune to others. I want to touch on some unique aspects of each of these as they relate to attunement and also introduce another barrier—the influence of the me culture.

Technology

We talked about multitasking in chapter 1, "The Indulgence of Sensuality"—about how our fast-paced world makes it challenging to stay present in our bodies, but I want to highlight the influence of technology as a component of multitasking. It is this element of modern society that makes it so challenging to practice attunement on a regular basis.

Activities that previously took place in person, such as meetings or interviews, are increasingly happening via videoconferencing or over the phone. You can learn just about anything via an online course, so why bother signing up for an in-person class? The potential negative consequences of these changes are perhaps most strongly felt in the development of romantic relationships that begin online. When I am counseling a client who is braving the digital waters of online dating, I make it a point to encourage him or her to meet that potential partner in person sooner rather than later. It is not uncommon for my clients to tell me that they are getting the *sense* that a strong rapport or even chemistry is beginning to develop with a potential partner via flirty messages and winking emojis. This can continue for quite some time until the couple decides to meet in person. Many of these same people are then surprised to find that the chemistry they had been sure would follow from extended periods of time spent winking, messaging, texting, and perhaps even a phone call or two falls flat when they meet their online matches in person. When they ask me why this is, I explain to them that the reason has a lot to do with attunement.

Much is missed when texting, emailing, and videoconferencing are our only forms of communication. Despite the availability of a wide variety of emojis, GIFs, memes, and other graphic delights, it is easy to misconstrue a person's tone or miss an intended inflection when we cannot directly read someone's body language and emotional expression the way we can in physical proximity. You might say that we don't just see and hear others when we are physically near them, we *feel* them—their "presence," "energy," or "vibe." This can be described as all that is both quantifiable and unquantifiable about a person, encompassing the way they smell, the texture and color of their physical characteristics, the touch of their hand, or the unaltered sound of their voice. Without being physically present with someone, our mirror neurons have a much harder time picking up on all the information needed to form an adequate connection. It is as if the cognitive connection created via messaging is too far attenuated for a true emotional connection to form, which can drastically throw off our perception.

Upon further exploration, I learned this was the primary way that Sloane and Cameron had communicated, especially over the last ten years. Given their demanding jobs and travel schedules, it wasn't uncommon for most of their communication to happen via text and email. They reported feeling like two ships passing in the night. Dinners (only a fraction of which happened together) usually consisted of takeout they ate quickly while simultaneously checking emails. They even admitted to working on most of their vacations together. They didn't realize how far apart they'd grown over the past several years despite sharing a roof and life goals. My first homework exercise for them was to sit and check in face-to-face without any distractions on a daily basis.

"You can use this check-in to talk about your day, address an issue, or make plans. And always try to express gratitude or an affirmation about each other," I instructed them. I encouraged them to hold hands and maintain eye contact as they spoke (much like I described in chapter 1) so that they could start to reattune to one another. It wasn't that they were never together, but the quality of their time together was severely lacking, making it impossible for them to be emotionally attuned.

As it relates to romantic relationships and sex, not only do we spend less time with our partners today than ever before,[2] but we rush through sex too. Virtual communication and limited in-person interactions make it harder for our bodies to attune to those close to us.

Attunement is an essential element of any relationship. Imagine how hard it is to comfort a friend you are on the phone with or texting instead of being able to hold them or intuit what they might need in person.

Gender Socialization

We touched on gender socialization previously, but I want to take a deeper dive here to illustrate how it inhibits our ability to attune. Innate gender differences as well as gender socialization can make some aspects of attunement easier for women than for men. While we are all hardwired for attunement, studies have found that women are biologically predisposed to be more empathic than men.[3] This may be because, traditionally, babies relied primarily on their mothers for survival, and survival includes the provision of food as well as tending to a baby's emotional needs or cries for help.[4] The male role was primarily to support the mother and provide food for the larger group.

Gender *socialization* most likely plays an even bigger role. From a very early age, boys are taught to suppress their emotions. They are encouraged to be competitive, to be decisive, and to problem-solve quickly. *Suck it up. No pain, no gain. Don't be a baby. Stop acting like such a sissy.* In contrast, girls are generally encouraged to express their emotions, to be nurturing of others, and to have strong interpersonal skills.[5] *Sweetheart, your little brother is crying. Why don't you see if he wants a hug? Chin up. Don't forget to smile. Be polite.* This can result in different relationship challenges for men and women. Through my work as a clinician, I have observed a distinct trend among the heterosexual couples that I counsel. Often, the challenge for men is to become more empathic and emotionally attuned to their female partners, whereas the goal for the women is to develop better ways of communicating their needs (e.g., learn that their partners are not mind readers) to male partners who may not be predisposed toward attunement.

When men see a problem or notice that their partner is in distress, it's not uncommon for them to automatically find a way to "fix it." However, attunement to your partner's emotional needs is quite different from fixing a physical object that is broken in one's house or solving a mathematical equation. Sometimes, the actions men will take to "solve the problem" only serve to exacerbate women's feelings of being unheard, which is the last thing needed in those types of situations.

A humorous dramatization of such an exchange can be found in the classic 1990s film *White Men Can't Jump*. In one scene, a couple, Gloria and Billy, lies together in bed one morning. Gloria tells Billy that she is thirsty. Billy reacts by getting up from the bed to bring her a glass of water. To his utter confusion, she is not satisfied with this and tells him, "When I said I was thirsty, it doesn't mean I want a glass of water . . . You're missing the whole point of me saying I'm thirsty. If I have a problem, you're not supposed to solve it. Men always make the mistake of thinking they can solve a woman's problem . . . I don't want a glass of water, I want you to sympathize. I want you to say, 'Gloria, I too know what it feels like to be thirsty. I too have had a dry mouth.' I want you to connect with me through sharing and understanding the concept of dry-mouthed-ness.'"

Granted, this scene is a bit ridiculous, but Gloria is using the moment as an opportunity to explain a larger problem in the couple's relationship—that Billy keeps trying to "fix" things when what she really wants is attunement. Billy, who has likely been conditioned since childhood to put feelings aside, solve problems, and "get the job done," is utterly confused and frustrated by her response. "When I say I'm thirsty, it means if anybody has a glass of water, I'd love a sip!" he exclaims.

While it may be humorous to watch this exchange in a movie, these types of conflicts are very real and can have very serious consequences for many couples. This is why such a large percentage of couples' communication skills techniques start with mirroring exercises, which are designed to deepen empathy and understanding. The From Old Perceptions to New Perspectives exercise from chapter 2 had some mirroring worked into it. Each time Partner B is prompted to parrot back what Partner A said, it is to help them slow down and attune to what Partner A has just communicated before jumping to a quick defense or solution. Slowing down, a concept we will come back to a few times throughout this chapter, is one of the best ways of helping our bodies and hearts sync up so that we can be more highly attuned.

This kind of dialoguing serves several purposes. When confronted with a problem, it's not uncommon for a listener's defenses to go up quickly, which inhibits our ability to really *hear* and *feel* them. If you feel threatened or accused, you may prepare your rebuttal before your partner has even finished telling you the full extent of the problem. Even if a problem could be solved through some type of decisive action, the proper action cannot be taken if you don't have all the information you need. To be attuned is to allow your partner to speak openly while you listen attentively to the complete story they are telling you. It's important to not only listen intently to what they tell you about their emotions and confirm what you have heard but also to pay attention to their body language. This in itself is profound—the simple act of letting your partner know that they have been heard, that you now see the full scope of their problem, and that you understand their true feelings—can make a huge improvement in any relationship.

By pausing to share, repeat, and confirm your understanding of the problem and of the feelings that your partner associates with the problem, you can better understand the emotional piece of the puzzle before jumping too quickly to a solution or taking some type of action that might only make matters worse. The link between our thoughts, feelings, and behaviors is one that we will explore in greater detail later in this chapter. By stating and repeating your feelings and emotions aloud together as a couple, you will strengthen the pathways of emotional attunement between you and your partner. With time and practice, partners can eventually learn to attune to each other quite naturally.

Family of Origin

The family-of-origin stories I learned from Sloane and Cameron illustrated how gender socialization and attachment likely played a role in their ability to attune to each other.[6]

Cameron's father worked for long periods of time overseas, leaving his mother alone to take care of three children. When his father was home, things were relatively peaceful, but when he was away, his mother became overwhelmed. This created an inconsistent environment, where his mother's emotions would vacillate between extremes. It was common for her to lose her temper at even the slightest prompting, secluding herself in her room, leaving Cameron to take care of himself and his younger siblings. As the eldest child, Cameron recognized that it was difficult for his mother to manage three children alone, and he adjusted his behavior accordingly. It didn't take long for Cameron to assume the role of peacekeeper in the household, especially during times when his father was away. As time went on,

Cameron learned to ignore his mother's mood swings, doing whatever he had to do to keep things happy and light until his father returned.

Tragically, when Sloane was eight years old, she lost her mother to cancer. This caused a profound shift in her family life that is still felt many years later. Shortly after her mother's passing, Sloane's father battled periods of depression and heavy drinking. Like Cameron, Sloane was the oldest of three children, and as the only girl, she felt a responsibility to care for her younger siblings and provide emotional support to her father. However, in sharp contrast to Cameron's learned ability to ignore his mother's mood swings, Sloane developed an overly sensitive attunement to her father's often precarious emotional states. She was especially mindful of preventing him from slipping into depression or consuming alcohol. Telltale warning signs of his pending relapse included observations that the family's laundry was piling up, that her father had stayed late at work, or that he did not engage with his children during dinner. As a result, Sloane became hyperaware of any changes in her father's body language, tone, or behavior that might signal that he was about to slip.

Perhaps not surprisingly, Cameron's emotional *disconnect* and Sloane's emotional *hypersensitivity* created conflict in their relationship. Now that both Sloane and Cameron had more time on their hands, Sloane constantly accused Cameron of not making their relationship a priority and worried incessantly that he was in a bad mood. He was quick to rebuff her attempts to connect and at times acted aloof, which only made her more anxious. It wasn't just verbal communication that they struggled with, it was emotional attunement. This is why standard communication exercises only take people so far in therapy. When I work with clients like Sloane and Cameron, I strive to teach them how to attune to each other's nonverbal emotional cues more appropriately, a skill I'll outline further into this chapter.

Think about your own family of origin. You may have grown up in a family in which you felt your caregivers ignored or dismissed your emotional needs. Perhaps you felt they were too busy to deal with you. This may have left you with a core belief that your needs don't truly matter and that it's better to just ignore them. On the other hand, you may have grown up in an environment in which you had to be hyper-attuned to the emotional needs of one or more of your caregivers. Thus, your "emotional radar" may be on high alert at all times. Living in either extreme can make it difficult to have a positive relationship with your own emotional needs, let alone healthy attunement to your partner. This can have major relationship and sexual consequences. What I find interesting about these two extremes is that they both focus on the self. People who are hyposensitive or emotionally disconnected from others tend to be more self-absorbed, while people who are hypersensitive tend to be self-conscious. This focus on the self is perhaps no more evident than in modern-day culture, a.k.a. me culture, which is the last barrier I want to explore.

Me Culture

Me culture can be best described as the age of individualism that has become so predominant in recent years. It's hard to pinpoint exactly when this shift happened, but it's likely built into Western (and particularly American) cultural ideology.

More than in other countries, there is a focus on individualism here in the United States. Look around the rest of the globe, and you're far more likely to find multiple generations of families living under one roof. Small villages in other parts of the world are built densely compared to the sprawling suburbanism we see here in the United States. These sorts of living conditions and cultures in other countries set people up to think more communally. They are attuned to the group as opposed to the individual.

That's not what we see here in the United States. Now more than ever, I see posts and articles glorifying singledom and touting more self-care as the answer to all our woes. Considering the needs of others is pathologized as codependent. We are quick to label people as toxic and cancel them from our lives. At no point in history has there ever been a greater focus on one's self. At no point in history has there been a greater mental health and relationship crisis.[7] Coincidence? I think not. The focus on individual needs creates major problems for couples. Rather than externalizing conflicts and thinking about how couples can work as a team to solve them, my clients view relationship conflict through the lens of two opposing individual needs. In other words, it becomes about "my needs versus your needs" rather than "our needs" as a couple.

We forget that humans, as a species, are social. We evolved to be interdependent and to rely on one another through emotional attunement and collaboration. As we reach adulthood, we eventually gain the ability to take care of most of our own emotional needs, but that doesn't mean we don't still need other people too. When it comes to adult relationships, our capacity for intimacy and closeness still largely depends upon our ability to tune in and respond to the emotional states of those around us. Higher levels of attunement and empathy lead to higher degrees of closeness, compassion, intimacy, and, ultimately, passion, in our relationships.[8]

The mirror neurons I described before don't suddenly turn off when we become self-sufficient. If you've ever noticed yourself wince when you see your friend get a paper cut, you'll realize that your mirror neurons are still very much active. In these cases, looking at your friend evokes an emotional and physical response from you as a viewer. In this way, we as viewers begin to embody what we see in the world around us.

In chapter 1, the focus of the material was designed to cultivate the embodiment of *oneself*. In this chapter, we are now ready to learn how to externalize that awareness and employ our skills to more fully embody *another person's* experience while at the same time staying connected to our own bodies. This kind of attuned embodiment is an essential component in your connectedness to others and a key secret in cultivating a passionate sexual experience.

DISCOVERING ATTUNEMENT WITHIN YOURSELF

Our ability to tune in to others is greatly enhanced when we first tune in to ourselves. Just as tuning in to others is about recognizing and responding to emotional states, body language, and tone, tuning in to ourselves begins with fine-tuning our awareness of and response to our own emotions, thoughts, and body sensations. This type of "self-attunement" prevents us from living life on autopilot. This means fine-tuning our awareness of the thoughts, feelings, and behaviors we exhibit on a daily basis, a process referred to as *mindfulness*. If we return to our dancing analogy from before, this is about taking lessons by yourself to learn the basics before trying your moves out with a partner.

Having explored how to tune in to our bodies' sensations in chapter 1 and how to open our minds in chapter 2, we will now expand those principles to include information on how to connect our bodies and minds to our behaviors. Our thoughts, feelings, and behaviors are intertwined, and each affects the others. Many of our behaviors stem from automatic reactions—instinctive responses that we experience every day but typically are not fully conscious of because we are out of tune with ourselves. Through these reactions, our patterns of engaging with the world can become so deeply ingrained that they happen automatically. Many of us don't realize how much of our automatic behavior, especially as it relates to sex, is shaped from our formative years or from gender socialization. We touched on this in chapter 2—about how important it is to question our automatic thoughts about things—and I want to take it a bit further here. Authenticity, or understanding ourselves for who we would be had it not been for our early experiences, cannot be reached until we begin to unpack these impulsive responses. To do this, we must pay attention to the stories we tell ourselves and "look at ourselves in the mirror" to examine who we really are.

Most people have a strong emotion and behave in re-action to the feeling without questioning it. As I began to understand where things went off course for Sloane and Cameron, it became apparent that this was part of the problem.

"Walk me through a typical sexual experience. What works well, and when do things start to feel awkward?" I prompted.

Cameron cleared his throat. "It's easy to get lost in the kiss. It's just the right amount of tongue. Every now and then, Sloane nibbles my lip, which I love. I could make out with her for hours."

"That sounds wonderful," I replied. "Now tell me where things fall apart when you take things further."

"Well," he began, "once our careers took off, we stopped prioritizing our sexual relationship. We had sex, but it was usually quick and to the point, if you will. We were just too busy to care. Now that we are trying to connect more inten-tionally, we're going slowly and figuring out what feels good. We've read up on sexual communication, and I'm trying to voice my desires." He hesitated. "I don't think I'm asking for anything too wild and crazy, but I'd love for Sloane to go down on me. I'm older than I was when we got together, and the extra stimulation really helps. Anytime we try, she gets awkward and uncomfortable, which kills the mood for both of us. I don't want her to feel that way, obviously. I would never push her to do something she didn't want to do, but I feel like we are limited in our repertoire. To me, it's one of many things that feels intimate, and I'd like to understand why she feels different. We need some guidance. This is part of what makes sex so awkward for us now. Not only are we misaligned in our beliefs about what is enjoyable, we fumble through the act as if we have no experience."

Sloane and Cameron had failed to adapt as careers took over and the effects of aging set in. I explained the importance of adaptability, highlighting the key points I described in chapter 3. Then I turned to Sloane to get her side of the story. "Tell me what bothers you about giving oral sex," I prompted.

Sloane rolled her eyes. "To me, giving head is anti-feminist. I didn't get to where I am by getting down on my knees for a man."

Without looking up from the floor, Cameron added, "Sloane, you know I don't think that way of you. I have so much respect for you and don't at all see this as something that is in opposition to that."

It was clear Sloane was having a strong automatic reaction. I wanted to help her exercise curiosity about her reaction so that she could more finely attune to her own experience and ultimately find a way to tune in to Cameron.

"Would it be okay if we explored your feelings about oral sex?" I asked. "When you think about going down on Cameron, what emotion comes up for you?" I asked.

"Emotion? I'm not really sure. I just don't want to."

"Let's try this," I started. "Close your eyes and bring your awareness to your body. Tune in to the sensations you're experiencing and tell me what you notice." This question was designed to help her strengthen attunement to herself. I wanted to know what signals her body was sending her and why.

"I feel a pit in my stomach."

"A pit in the stomach usually signifies shame or even disgust. Does that seem like the right fit for what you experience?"

Sloane nodded.

"Okay," I said. "So we can identify three components—the thoughts, feelings, and behavior—of what the experience is like for you. The thought is, *Giving oral is anti-feminist*, the emotion is shame, and the behavior is avoidance of the act. Does that sum it up?"

She nodded again.

"Okay, now for the fun part. I want you to attune more consciously and mindfully to the experience itself and to the thoughts and feelings associated with it, then ask yourself two important questions. The first is *what evidence you have to support the idea that oral sex is anti-feminist*, and the second is *what evidence you have to refute the idea that oral sex is anti-feminist*." I hoped her background as a lawyer would make the evidence-seeking part interesting.

"Several things come to mind when I think of evidence in support of my thought. One is what I see in porn. Nothing about that speaks to female empowerment. Second is that it's about his pleasure and not mine, so it doesn't feel equal."

"Okay, fair enough. Now tell me what evidence you can come up with in refute of the idea."

She looked at me with a blank stare.

"Let me pose some questions to get the ball rolling," I said.

"What about oral sex in same-sex couples? What about the fact that this is happening within the context of a loving relationship as opposed to two strangers meeting for the first time on a porn set? What about the fact that during oral sex, you have one of your strongest body parts—your jaw—around one of his most sensitive body parts and that he's putting total faith and trust in you to make it a pleasurable experience?" I glanced at Cameron. Now he was the one recoiling.

"I hadn't thought about it like that before," she admitted.

"Take a moment and sit with the feelings that are coming up for you now," I told her. "Can you replace the thought *Oral sex is antifeminist* with an alternative or more balanced thought? Because right now, your feelings and behavior about oral sex are happening automatically based on a thought that we have now challenged. Let's see what new thought we can come up with and explore how your feelings and behavior change," I explained.

She thought for a moment. Cameron looked at her expectantly.

"How's this?" she said. "Despite the pleasure being more focused on Cameron in that moment, it is still a moment of intimacy and mutual trust."

"I love that," I told her. "Now, tune in to yourself again and see how your feelings have changed. How's that sensation in your stomach?"

"I don't have the pit in my stomach anymore. When you describe it like that, it kind of does sound empowering in a weird way. Maybe I have more control than I originally thought. And the fact that he's trusting me in such a vulnerable moment is kind of sweet."

"What would happen if we took 'control' out of the equation altogether and instead framed it as one of many components of a shared sexual experience? There are plenty of moments when pleasure is shared and other moments when the focus is a bit more on one person than the other. The important thing is that you feel like there is an equal distribution of pleasure overall," I told her.

"I suppose I'd be open to trying it again now that I'm thinking about it differently," she said.

"I think that's a good place to start."

Cameron smiled broadly.

I explained to them how focusing on their body sensations and identifying their feelings (chapter 1) as well as actively exploring their automatic thoughts and beliefs (chapter 2), finding the pockets of trust and connection (chapter 4), and being willing to try again (chapter 3) all led to a more finely attuned experience. It is only with this level of attunement that we can more fully surrender to the bliss that comes from great sex.

When it comes to sex, we haul everything that's been inculcated into us to the experience. Part of learning to tune in and be fully authentic in your sexual expression is examining and letting go of unhelpful, incorrect, or destructive thoughts and feelings. Use the next exercise to explore what you may be bringing to the table.

Tuning in to Your Thoughts, Feelings, and Behaviors

Challenge your automatic reactions by completing the chart below.

What is the situation you're reacting to?	
What emotion do you notice most strongly? How intense is the feeling? (0–10)	
What automatic thought(s) do you have about the situation and your emotions?	
How strongly do you believe your automatic thought? (0–10)	
What evidence do you have that supports the automatic thought?	
What evidence do you have that refutes the automatic thought? (Consider the following: What would you say to a friend who had that automatic thought? Have you ever had an experience that would suggest that thought is not true? Are you jumping to conclusions with that thought?)	
Write down an alternative or balanced thought. How much do you believe the new thought? (0–10)	
What emotion do you feel now? How strong is the new feeling? (0–10) What can you do differently?	

I encouraged Sloane and Cameron to use this protocol to challenge their reactivity in other situations too. Their family-of-origin experiences paired with their lifestyles as adults had them going on autopilot. With time, practice, and checking in regularly with each other using the tools I gave them, they noticed a drastic reduction in their bickering. As a bonus, they saw and understood themselves as individuals in a new and deeper way. Sex still wasn't where they wanted it to be, but they had begun the process of internal attunement by becoming more mindful of their inner thoughts and feelings and understanding the effect on their behavior. Now it was time to extend those skills to their relationship.

CREATING ATTUNEMENT IN YOUR RELATIONSHIP

Two-way attunement within a relationship can only happen if you're committed to working *with* your partner as opposed to against them. I touched on this in the "Barriers to Attunement" section—about how attuned couples work together to solve problems rather than getting trapped in the "my needs versus your needs" stance. Sloane was guilty of this when she saw Cameron's desire for oral sex as a selfish need as opposed to something that had the potential to benefit them both. Teamwork is important for any meaningful relationship, whether it's with your colleagues or your children and especially with your significant other. Couples who experience a lack of attunement often use phrases like, "I feel disconnected, shut out, unheard, and unseen," whereas couples who are tuned in to each other use phrases like, "I feel like we're in sync, on the same page, deeply connected, and understood."

Relationship scientist Dr. John Gottman's definition of attunement can be a good way to start conceptualizing attunement in relationships.[9] He created a great acronym that makes it easy to remember. The essence of attunement, he says, is the following:

Awareness
Turning toward
Tolerance
Understanding
Nondefensive responding
Empathy

Awareness refers to having a knowledge of your partner's inner and outer world. This is intimacy and curiosity. *Turning toward* refers to your willingness to connect when your partner reaches out as well as your emotional availability when you *sense* they may need you. *Tolerance* means creating space for them to express emotion as well as soothing your own uncomfortable emotions. This is differentiation, if you recall from chapter 4, "The Intensity of Vulnerability." *Understanding* refers to your ability to get what your partner's emotional experience is like. *Nondefensive* partners suspend their immediate reaction to ensure they grasp what their partners may be trying to communicate. We learned how to do this in chapter 3, "The Power of Adaptability."

And finally, partners who respond empathically *show* they understand their loved ones through behavior that reflects that understanding. They don't just talk the talk; they walk the walk.

When well-attuned couples sense a drift, they refocus, reconnect, and re-devote themselves to each other. In short, well-attuned couples don't lose their relationship flow, and they find it much easier to slip into erotic flow.

Relational attunement has been demonstrated in parent-child relationships, therapist-client interactions, teammates, friends, and, of course, romantic couples. Being in sync is a real biological phenomenon. The nervous systems of highly attuned couples quite literally sync up with each other. Researchers refer to this as *physiological synchrony*. If one person's heart rate escalates, the other person's follows. If one person's breathing slows, the other's does too. Research finds that couples with higher-quality relationships and higher empathy have greater physiological synchrony compared to couples who are dissatisfied in their relationship.[10] A more recent study found an interesting link between sexual satisfaction and physiological synchrony.[11] The researchers measured couples' heart rates across three conditions—one in which they sat facing each other with blindfolds on, one in which they were instructed to gaze into each other's eyes, and a third in which they were vaguely told to mirror each other's gestures. For example, if one person crossed their arms, the other was supposed to do the same. Findings indicated that couples with higher sexual satisfaction synced up significantly more during the mirroring condition compared to couples with lower sexual satisfaction. An interesting detail of these findings is that women's heart rates tended to follow their male partners' heart rates presumably because (as we discussed before) women are often more adept at reading nonverbal cues than men.

When we are attuned to our partners, it is as if we enter into a dance—much like the example I began this chapter with. Attunement allows us to *respond* to our partners in beneficial ways, as opposed to *reacting* in ways that might not be helpful. Being highly attuned takes pressure off verbal communication. Don't get me wrong—we need to be good verbal communicators, especially about important issues, but at some point, we need to learn our partners' nonverbal cues as well.

Now that Sloane and Cameron had attuned to their internal experiences, they were ready to start discovering each other's nonverbal worlds. At this point in our work together, I wondered if Sloane and Cameron were as misaligned as they thought. I asked them to tell me more about how they functioned as a couple in relation to supporting each other's careers.

"I think that part has been relatively easy," Sloane said. "I'm probably better at reading Cameron's pulse when he needs to focus at the office, but he does a good job of stepping back when I need to work extra hours. It's rare that we have conflict around work stuff. I always just assumed that part of our relationship was easy since we don't have kids to juggle in the mix."

"Sloane!" I said excitedly. "I love that phrase you just used—that you're good at reading his pulse. That is exactly what attunement is all about. Let's take that skill and see if we can transfer it to the emotional and sexual domain of your relationship." I gave them the following exercise.

Relational Attunement

Sit face-to-face with your partner. Avoid bulky clothing, as it will make it harder to tune in to each other's bodies.

Hold your partner's hand with one of your hands and rest the other hand gently over their heart.

With your eyes open, watch the rhythmic rise and fall of each other's breathing and feel the pulse of each other's hearts.

Now, bring your attention to your own breathing and heart rate.

Switch your attention back and forth between your partner's body and your own. Notice their facial expression and see if you can get a read on the emotions and body sensations they may be experiencing. Then do the same for yourself.

See if at any point you can hold awareness for both you and your partner simultaneously.

If you laugh or start to feel awkward, just take a deep breath and try to refocus. Stay with this for at least five minutes and then discuss the experience with your partner.

This little exercise was transformational for Sloane and Cameron. Individual attunement had worked as a stepping stone, but it wasn't enough to help them rediscover their rhythm as a couple. Relational attunement, which they only needed each other for, is what started to guide them home. I encourage couples to do this exercise when they are feeling out of sync in their relationship. I find it to be a quick and effective way of calming the body and syncing up with our partners' nervous systems.

Only with deeper self and other awareness can you become truly *emotionally intelligent*, a skill that anybody is adept to learn. In the 1990s, the concepts in psychologist Dr. Daniel Goleman's book *Emotional Intelligence* gained wide popularity. Essentially, emotional intelligence is the notion that you can recognize, identify, and respond to feelings within yourself and in others and use this information to strengthen your relationships, adapt to your environment, and achieve your goals.[12] For example, have you ever walked into a room and felt like you could cut the tension with a knife? You may have noticed a person's rigid posture, squinted eyes, curt tones, or defensive body language. Perhaps the energy in the room created a tension within you as well, giving you the urge to exit as quickly as possible.

In contrast, have you ever seen a happy couple at a nearby table while you were dining out? Have you noticed that they mimic each other's behaviors? When one takes a sip of wine, the other likely follows; when one scratches the side of his head, the other fluffs their hair; when one relaxes into their chair, the other sits back as well. This is an interesting phenomenon in which two people subconsciously mirror each other's gestures, body posture, or even style of speaking. This is a good sign of two people being attuned and in sync.

This is emotional intelligence: your ability to pick up on body language, tone of voice, facial expressions, energy, and even breathing. It's a skill people need to master not only in their relationships but in the bedroom as well. Think back to the examples I shared at the beginning of the chapter—the clients who complained of their partners' lack of sexual attunement. Like Sloane and Cameron, we stop being emotionally intelligent and attuned as soon as the clothes come off. We become so focused on meeting our own needs or doing what we *think* our partners *should* like that we forget to stop and read the room (or in this case, our partners' bodies and nonverbal cues). Our and our partners' bodies hold a rich world of information that will guide us if we learn to pay attention. When we open our eyes and stop rushing through sex, we'll notice subtle shifts in facial expression, muscle tension, and breathing that can give us wonderful clues about our partners' pleasure. Learning to read and respond to these subtle shifts means we don't have to interrupt our own internal experience by vocalizing what we want or asking if something feels good. This is a skill that only attuned lovers know and understand. Imagine if players on a sports team had to stop and talk through every move. They'd never win! Couples stop acting like a team because they become disconnected from themselves and each other.

Think of a pair of tennis doubles. Typically, the game is happening so rapidly that the doubles team hardly has time to think. They must learn how to quickly and effectively work together to get the ball back over the net. As tennis coach Ron Waite described, "When coaching tennis,

I have actually tied a rope around the waist of two doubles partners. If this team is moving as one, the rope will always remain taut, but never result in either player being pulled off balance." Spectators can tell when a doubles team has been playing together for a long time because they seem to move as one unit. The same applies to couples.

Furthermore, like any successful team, couples must practice. I cannot emphasize this point enough. The less often you do something, the less skilled you'll be. The same principle applies to emotional, relational, and sexual attunement. If you rarely spend quality time together or don't have sex with relative frequency, you cannot expect to be finely tuned. Think of tuning an instrument. You can pick it up and enjoy playing it several times before having to stop and retune it. If left unattended for long periods, you'll have to go through the re-attunement each time, which will make it harder to slip into flow when you play.

Direct verbal communication is an important part of practice, but eventually, you have to learn to trust your body and your body's response to your partner. I think this is where so many couples get hung up. They do the communication training, but then allow too much time to pass before practicing again. Or they let feelings of awkwardness (which comes when you haven't done something in a while) stop them from trying again. Practice is an essential element of mastering any skill, and that includes attunement. With time, like a pair of successful tennis doubles, you won't have to stop and verbally discuss every little play. You can hit the court (or jump into bed) and let attunement take over.

It's interesting because most couples start out feeling like a highly attuned team. Think of the rituals involved in various types of wedding ceremonies. Depending upon the type of wedding, the ceremony officiant will most often prompt the bride and groom to engage in a variety of customs that encourage bonding and attunement: you must gaze at each other, kneel together, break a glass together, exchange sacred words with each other, and a whole variety of other rituals that, while variable in different cultures and religions, overall serve to orchestrate attunement and bonding.

Of course, weddings and marriages are not required for strong bonds, but I find it curious how relationships in their early stages, and these ceremonial rituals in particular, are all about attunement. Most couples start out with the best of intentions, yet many are not able to sustain the levels of attunement necessary to keep the bonds of their relationship going strong. It is as if their attunement becomes lost in the weedy landscape that day-to-day life can become. In our partnerships, if we can make a conscious effort to keep these bonding rituals, like sharing a morning coffee, kissing before work, or holding each other before drifting off to sleep, then we are cultivating long-lasting attunement that can support us in the relationship and the bedroom.

CULTIVATING ATTUNEMENT IN EROTICISM

Okay, my friends. This is where it all comes together. This is how you reach nirvana. You already have the basic tools to reach erotic flow. Understanding how to experience embodiment, how to open your mind and your heart, and how to adapt to the ebbs and flows of life puts you more than halfway there. But this is where it gets really good. This is where you'll take it to the next level. I've talked about how to use your higher-order thinking skills to cultivate great sex. We use our brains to plan, communicate effectively, and make decisions about what needs to be in place for sex to be highly satisfying. But now I'm going to talk about how *quieting* the brain—which can only happen when you're fully attuned to your partner—will help you slip into a truly optimal sexual connection. What I'm about to describe is the ultimate expression of erotic attunement. This last bit will help you feel in sync the way Miguel and I did on the dance floor back at Gloria's all those years ago.

Something very cool happens when we are in a state of flow—a phenomenon referred to as *transient hypofrontality*.[13] I'll explain what that means in a moment, but it is this neurological shift that gives us some of flow's greatest elements—altered perception of time (time may seem to speed up or slow down), merger of action and awareness (that feeling of being at one with whatever we're doing), and loss of self-consciousness (the chitter-chatter in our heads goes quiet).[14]

Let's break down the term *transient hypofrontality*. *Transient* means "temporary," *hypo* means "to slow down," and *frontality* refers to the prefrontal cortex of the brain. Thus, *transient hypofrontality* means that the prefrontal cortex of the brain temporarily quiets down. The prefrontal cortex sits just behind the forehead. This brain region controls higher-order cognitive skills, such as abstract thought, reasoning, decision-making, and planning. It's also where our personalities live, gives us our sense of time, and helps us differentiate between "self" and "other." It's not fully formed until we are about twenty-five years old. This explains why

some teenagers can be impulsive, run late, or have a dis-
regard for the impact of their actions on other people. But
isn't this mentality, to an extent, what we as adults long for,
especially during sex—that feeling of reckless abandon?

My research participant Henry certainly did. He explained that at sixty-eight years old, sex was one of the only
activities that made him feel young again. He emphasized
how sex was always where he and his wife rediscovered
each other through life's ups and downs. He described it
as "an escape—a recess from the grind of life," stating that
"sex is what keeps our relationship fresh despite the ever-
increasing wrinkles in our skin. It makes me forget everything else that's going on around me."

Another couple from my study, Leo and Maya, described
how sex gave them momentary windows of reckless abandon. Their adolescent son had learning differences and a
mood disorder. They described how tiring their day-to-day
lives were between the extra tutors and therapy sessions and
managing their son's behavior. But sex, they said, gave them
the opportunity to forget the stress and pressure they were
under. "'Adulting' is exhausting sometimes. Sex makes us
feel wild and free like we did before all these responsibilities
took over." They explained how it usually happened in the
middle of the night, when they were in that sweet, deeply
relaxed spot between sleep and wakefulness, that they could
surrender to each other's pleasure. "It's as if our bodies take
over," they said.

It was time for Sloane and Cameron to put everything
they'd learned about attunement to the test. I wanted to help
them reach flow the way my research participants described.
They mentioned that they'd exhausted every sexual com-

munication exercise, and now that they felt more in sync as a couple, I decided to suggest something different.

"I wonder what would happen if you forgot everything you've read," I said. "You can read up on techniques all day long, but at the end of the day, you're each other's best playbook."

I explained a Zen Buddhism philosophy known as *shoshin*, which encourages people to adopt a "beginner's mind."

"You're completely out of practice with each other. I think it's time you look at each other with a fresh set of eyes and a completely open mind." I explained that when we go into something thinking we are experts (as many people do after reading how-to books about sex), we are too cerebral. Trying to remember a technique we read about in a book prevents us from tuning in to the rich cues emanating from our partners. I reminded them of the importance of quieting the mind and explained how much more engaged with the senses we are when we are new at something.

"The next time you have sex, go slowly," I instructed. "Go at a snail's pace. Don't even think of sex as having a beginning, a middle, and an end. It may feel like it plateaus, but just know that you can pick up where you left off next time, and trust that with practice, the feeling of effortlessness and the bliss of a quiet mind will eventually come.

"Keep your eyes and ears open," I told them, "so that you can notice each other's breathing and focus on reading each other's nonverbal cues. Become aware of shifts in each other's bodies and notice what happens in your own body accordingly. I want to warn you that this is probably going to feel more awkward at first, but that's because I'm instructing you to learn each other in a way you haven't before. Keep at it. Move through the struggle phase"—recall from the introduction—"and give it time to unfold." We scheduled a follow-up session a few weeks later.

Since the prefrontal cortex houses your sense of self, it takes shutting it down for you to lose yourself. In other words, your sense of self as a unit apart from the world is suspended in time. Loss of self-consciousness is blissful. You know you're in this state when you feel like you're fully absorbed in an experience.

It's incredible because in this state, you're free from anxiety, self-doubt, worry, and rumination. I find it interesting that while it's the prefrontal cortex that makes us so human (animals don't have this brain function), shutting it down again is what can make us feel superhuman and fully alive. One of my research participants, Chloe, explained how sex made her forget her worry and even physical pain. She had chronic back pain from a car accident years prior and worried constantly about her flare-ups. There were some positions she and her wife, Ines, could no longer do, but they adapted. Ines took extra care in massaging Chloe so that she could relax and settle into her body. "It's one of the few times that I can stop worrying about being in pain," Chloe said. "It is such a sweet escape."

When we experience a loss of self-consciousness, what's happening is a *merger of action and awareness*. This is another one of Mihaly Csikszentmihalyi's eight components of flow. Since we are less self-aware, our awareness shifts *outward* into the action or experience itself. What this means is that you become one with whatever you're doing. The classic example is the surfer who describes feeling at one with the wave. Imagine a painter whose perspective shifts from the artist to the artistic expression or a skilled surgeon whose being morphs from the doctor to the procedure itself. This is the epitome of a human *being*. Large groups can experience this too. Imagine the last sold-out concert you went to. How did it feel when the entire stadium of people waved their hands back and forth in unison as the band jammed out? It's as if the band, the music, and the tens of thousands of people merged as one energetic being. If we can do this in solo activities or as a collective, surely we can do it during sex with our beloved.

Research suggests that loss of self-consciousness leads to even greater levels of sexual satisfaction and responsiveness for women compared to men.[15] In other words, this may be an even more important skill for women to master. Women who can experience a loss of self-consciousness enjoy greater sexual desire and enhanced arousal and find it easier to reach orgasm. These findings don't surprise me. Women have a harder time shutting down the brain, especially during sex. Furthermore, they are more likely to be self-conscious, particularly about their body image, and more anxious than men. Loss of self-consciousness is what can make us feel so incredibly liberated during optimal sex. It frees us from self-critique, judgment, and inner distraction.

One of my clients, Kathryn, had terrible body image issues after her pregnancies, which caused her to avoid sex as much as possible. While most therapists would work to improve her body image before working on reintegrating sex, I took a backdoor approach. I explained how reaching a state of flow could help her forget about her insecurities.

I coached her and her husband on how to apply flow techniques to their own sex life, and with time, she found that her belly no longer bothered her. "I may not get into a bikini ever again," she said, "but I finally don't care how I look during sex. The physical and emotional pleasure takes precedent."

Since the prefrontal cortex shuts down during flow, the never-ending chatterboxes in our heads finally go quiet. Gone are the thoughts: *Don't forget to register Sally for summer camp. I need to get a head start on the marketing report that's due next week. Am I going to be able to climax this time?* Instead, the brain is still and peaceful. When we are in flow, we don't use more of the brain; in a way, we use less of it.

I checked in with Sloane and Cameron a few weeks later to see how things were going.

"Wow. Just wow," Sloane said. "It didn't happen the first or even the second time, and I'll admit, we both felt frustrated. But the third time, we definitely noticed a shift."

"Yes!" Cameron jumped in. "I think we both thought we were ahead of the curve by reading up on sexual techniques, but you were right. We are each other's best playbooks. We were both too much in our heads, doing what we thought *should* feel good at the pace we thought we *should* be going, but we were totally out of touch with what each other truly needed and to our own inner experiences."

Sloane continued, "And my anxiety disappeared. I've been so hypervigilant—more so than usual—since this whole process started, trying to pay attention to all of Cameron's cues while learning more about my own automatic reactions. And while I recognize those as important preliminary steps, it felt incredible to forget for a moment, not just about all the techniques but about life and, of course, about my own anxieties."

I smiled at them. "Was it just for a moment? How long do you think you were together?" I asked.

Cameron jumped in. "That was the other interesting thing. We looked at the clock, and a full half hour had passed. It felt like a moment suspended in time, but obviously, it was longer."

Cameron and Sloane had experienced another incredible phenomenon that happens when the brain goes quiet—the distortion of time and space. When you're in flow, time may seem to speed up or slow down. If you're like most folks, you probably have your day scheduled down to the minute. I know I do. You wake up with an alarm, calendar alerts constantly ping on your phone, and you're expected to return emails within an allotted period of time. But when we're in flow, five minutes could feel like five hours. One hour might feel like mere seconds. You check the clock, shocked to see the time because you were too far removed from it during that blissful, heightened state of consciousness. I invited Sloane and Cameron to take note of everything they did to set themselves up to experience a state of flow. I encourage you to do the same in this final exercise.

Finding Your Sexual Flow

First, think of your environment. What needs to be in place so that you're more likely to access flow? Do you need freshly laundered sheets, dim lighting, or mood music?

Next, think about yourself. Think about the exercises you've done so far to access your innate sensuality, curiosity, vulnerability, and adaptability. How can you connect with these elements in a way that is more likely to trigger flow?

Third, consider your relationship. Do you and your partner need to discuss your goals for your next sexual experience? Do you need to have a conversation to help you feel more attuned to each other? Do you need to try something new as a couple to reinvigorate the relationship?

Once you've prepared yourself and your relationship, channel all that wonderful energy into your next shared sexual experience and notice what emerges.

As you think about the other elements of flow as I've described them in other sections of this book, you'll understand why attunement is the gestalt of everything we've learned so far. It combines everything that we've learned to create something bigger, something more. Attunement draws from sensuality in that it invites us to connect with the feelings and sensations in our own bodies as well as that of our partners. It pulls from curiosity in that it calls us to remain inquisitive about how our thoughts and feelings influence our behaviors. It incorporates what we learned about adaptability because it inspires us to evolve in unison with our partners. And finally, it harnesses elements of vulnerability in that it bids us to surrender to the experience. Attunement, encompassing everything else we've learned, is the last and final secret you need to experience erotic passion that stands the test of time.

CONCLUSION

Throughout this book, you've come to know several couples who, despite caring for each other a great deal, struggled to achieve the sort of sex they wanted and knew they had at one time been capable of. It makes sense. Between kids, a mortgage, and other responsibilities, adult life does threaten to distract us from meaningful sexual connection. But as each of these couples learned, that doesn't mean that sex has to stop or even decline in quality. In fact, we should do everything in our power to prevent that from happening. As you've learned, people who are sexually satisfied feel happier in their relationships, feel their lives are more meaningful, and even experience better physical and emotional health. I hope that by now you see sex not just as an opportunity to escape from the troubles of daily life but also as a place of self-expression, relationship connection, and of course— physical pleasure.

With the right tools and mindset, couples can cultivate far better sex than they had in the early days. Yes, the novelty of a new partner is exciting (anyone with a beating heart can experience that), but mind-blowing intensity (which these secrets help you tap into) can most definitely be discovered in the nuance of intimacy, closeness, and shared experience that comes with a long-term relationship. Great sex doesn't happen by accident or as a result of amazing chemistry alone. In fact, many of the components needed to reach a flow state during sex, such as a feeling of effortlessness or the disinhibition needed for surrender are easier to reach with someone you know intimately and feel comfortable with. Talk to couples who've figured it out, and you'll learn that fulfilling sex is a result of two people who are dedicated to understanding their own bodies and their partner's body at a deeper, more intuitive level. Couples who have great sex know that having a flexible, go-with-the-flow attitude prevents sexual hiccups from growing into major problems. They maintain curious, open minds about themselves, their partner(s), and the potential for sexual growth over time. Together, these qualities help couples surrender into a flow state during sex, enjoying blissful, synchronous sex over and over again throughout their relationship. With intention, patience, and practice, every couple can cultivate an extraordinary sexual connection that stands the test of time.

ACKNOWLEDGMENTS

Writing a book has been a dream of mine for as long as I can remember. As I reflect on the number of people who helped make that dream a reality, I am filled with an overwhelming sense of gratitude. I have been inspired by so many individuals in my life, both past and present. The imprints they left on my heart ignited the very passion I aim to share with my readers. I am incredibly thankful to each and every one of them.

I would like to begin by thanking my family, without whom this book would not have been possible. Your unwavering belief in me along with your support and encouragement kept me motivated throughout my writing journey. To my husband, Shahin Jamea, thank you for your unparalleled patience and for loving me exactly as I am. To my children, thank you for gifting me the highest purpose in my life and giving me a deeper understanding of the world. When you are ready, I hope this book shows you how to love. To my parents, who pushed me to use my voice, thank you for giving me the confidence to put my thoughts on paper. To Tara Porras, who pushed me outside my comfort zone and helped me grow the platform I needed to achieve this lifelong dream of authoring.

I'd like to thank my agent, Frank Weimann, who changed my life with a simple phone call. Looking back on it now, the initial proposal I sent Frank was a very *very* rough draft that could have easily been discarded, but he immediately saw its potential. Frank, your kindness and patience with this novice author will not soon be forgotten. To my brilliant and talented editor, Bryn Clark, your insight was integral in this process. Thank you for adding a measure of poetry to my prose and teaching me how to write along the way. To the entire team at Flatiron Books, thank you for designing my dream cover and for giving color to my vision.

I'd like to thank Dr. Barry McCarthy, who served as an advisor for the research upon which this book is based. I feel incredibly fortunate to have had a mentor as experienced and prolific as you. Thank you to my co-researchers, Leah McCaskill and Rachel Needle, for your indispensable contributions to my research project. Thank you to Dr. Tammy Nelson, whose writing class I took nearly seven years ago. I was dubious then about the value of my perspective on this subject matter, but your immediate enthusiasm gave me the reassurance and courage I needed to commit fully to this process.

To my early readers, my colleagues and friends—Kimberly Sharky, Beth Christopherson, Aneliza Ochoa, Maria Larsson Payne, and Laura Palmero—thank you for taking the time to read early drafts of my manuscript. Your feedback was invaluable in helping me shape this book.

I'd like to extend an extra special thanks to Dr. Stephen Snyder, who, in addition to reviewing my book proposal, generously offered mentorship and resources early in my publishing journey.

To my tribe, especially the "Albans Girls," the "Ave. C Girls," and "The Core 5," who shared in my excitement as I passed each and every milestone.

To the research participants who bravely shared their stories about how they sustain passion and for allowing me to share those stories with the world. Your stories were deeply personal and included details about trying times in your life, and I am eternally grateful. Thank you to my clients for including me on your journeys. It takes immense courage to sit across from a therapist and reveal your deepest vulnerabilities and insecurities. Thank you for trusting me to guide and support you in your healing.

Finally, thank you to my readers for having the faith that this book might help you love a little deeper.

SEXUAL LIKES AND DISLIKES

IDENTIFYING SEXUAL LIKES AND DISLIKES

If you've never shared your sexual preferences with your partner, now's your chance. Sometimes we don't know how to articulate our likes and dislikes, and sometimes there are things we've never even considered. This exercise should help jump-start that conversation. Note that this is divided into GIVING, RECEIVING, MUTUAL, POSITIONS, and SOLO. Take your time with this exercise.

GIVING TO YOUR PARTNER

ACTIVITY	WE CURRENTLY DO IT	I WANT TO DO IT MORE	I DEFINITELY WANT TO TRY IT	I MIGHT CONSIDER TRYING IT	I DEFINITELY WON'T TRY IT
Caressing body (excluding breasts and genitals)	O	O	O	O	O
Caressing whole body	O	O	O	O	O
Looking into eyes	O	O	O	O	O
Licking (specify body part—e.g., genitals, anus, nipples, ears)	O	O	O	O	O
Sucking (specify body part)	O	O	O	O	O
Biting (specify body part)	O	O	O	O	O
Scratching with nails	O	O	O	O	O
Vaginal penetration with (specify fingers, mouth, tongue, penis, sex toy)	O	O	O	O	O

ACTIVITY	WE CURRENTLY DO IT	I WANT TO DO IT MORE	I DEFINITELY WANT TO TRY IT	I MIGHT CONSIDER TRYING IT	I DEFINITELY WON'T TRY IT
Anal penetration with *(specify fingers, mouth, tongue, penis, sex toy)*	O	O	O	O	O
Spanking partner	O	O	O	O	O
Tying partner up	O	O	O	O	O
Blindfolding partner	O	O	O	O	O
Other	O	O	O	O	O

RECEIVING FROM PARTNER

ACTIVITY	WE CURRENTLY DO IT	I WANT TO DO IT MORE	I DEFINITELY WANT TO TRY IT	I MIGHT CONSIDER TRYING IT	I DEFINITELY WON'T TRY IT
Caressing body *(excluding breasts and genitals)*	O	O	O	O	O
Caressing whole body	O	O	O	O	O
Looking into eyes	O	O	O	O	O

ACTIVITY	WE CURRENTLY DO IT	I WANT TO DO IT MORE	I DEFINITELY WANT TO TRY IT	I MIGHT CONSIDER TRYING IT	I DEFINITELY WON'T TRY IT
Licking (specify body part—e.g., genitals, anus, nipples, ears)	○	○	○	○	○
Sucking (specify body part)	○	○	○	○	○
Biting (specify body part)	○	○	○	○	○
Scratching with nails	○	○	○	○	○
Vaginal penetration with (specify fingers, mouth, tongue, penis, sex toy)	○	○	○	○	○
Anal penetration with (specify fingers, mouth, tongue, penis, sex toy)	○	○	○	○	○
Spanking partner	○	○	○	○	○
Tying partner up	○	○	○	○	○
Blindfolding partner	○	○	○	○	○
Other	○	○	○	○	○

MUTUAL ACTIVITIES

ACTIVITY	WE CURRENTLY DO IT	I WANT TO DO IT MORE	I DEFINITELY WANT TO TRY IT	I MIGHT CONSIDER TRYING IT	I DEFINITELY WON'T TRY IT
French kissing	O	O	O	O	O
Taking a bath or shower together	O	O	O	O	O
Sex in bathtub or shower together	O	O	O	O	O
Sex outside	O	O	O	O	O
Exhibitionism/ voyeurism	O	O	O	O	O
Face sitting	O	O	O	O	O
Shaving each other's pubic areas	O	O	O	O	O
Role-playing (specify)	O	O	O	O	O
Watching porn together / homemade porn	O	O	O	O	O
Slow sex	O	O	O	O	O
Strap-on play	O	O	O	O	O

ACTIVITY	WE CURRENTLY DO IT	I WANT TO DO IT MORE	I DEFINITELY WANT TO TRY IT	I MIGHT CONSIDER TRYING IT	I DEFINITELY WON'T TRY IT
Tantric sex	O	O	O	O	O
Masturbating while partner watches	O	O	O	O	O
Reading erotica together	O	O	O	O	O
Threesome	O	O	O	O	O
Group sex	O	O	O	O	O
BDSM	O	O	O	O	O
Erotic asphyxiation	O	O	O	O	O
Masturbating together	O	O	O	O	O
Sharing fantasies	O	O	O	O	O
Nonmonogamy (specify parameters)	O	O	O	O	O
Other	O	O	O	O	O

POSITIONS

ACTIVITY	WE CURRENTLY DO IT	I WANT TO DO IT MORE	I DEFINITELY WANT TO TRY IT	I MIGHT CONSIDER TRYING IT	I DEFINITELY WON'T TRY IT
Missionary	○	○	○	○	○
Woman on top (sitting)	○	○	○	○	○
Side-by-side facing	○	○	○	○	○
Side-by-side spooning	○	○	○	○	○
Reverse cowgirl	○	○	○	○	○
Doggy-style	○	○	○	○	○
Sixty-nine	○	○	○	○	○
Coital alignment technique	○	○	○	○	○
Other	○	○	○	○	○

SOLO ACTIVITIES

ACTIVITY	I CURRENTLY DO IT	I WANT TO DO IT MORE	I DEFINITELY WANT TO TRY IT	I MIGHT CONSIDER TRYING IT	I DEFINITELY WON'T TRY IT
Fantasizing	○	○	○	○	○
Reading erotica alone	○	○	○	○	○
Watching porn alone	○	○	○	○	○
Masturbating alone	○	○	○	○	○
Other	○	○	○	○	○

INITIATING SEX

I like it when you . . .

_____

_____

_____

_____

I like to initiate sex by . . .

_____

_____

_____

_____

TALKING DURING SEX

I like my genitals to be referred to as . . .

_____

_____

_____

_____

When it comes to talking during sex, I like . . .

_____

_____

_____

_____

LUBE

My thoughts on lube are . . .

_____

_____

_____

_____

OTHER

Use this blank space to make any additional notes.

_____

_____

_____

_____

_____

_____

_____

_____

_____

_____

_____

_____

_____

_____

_____

_____

_____

_____

_____

_____

_____

_____

_____

_____

_____

_____

_____

_____

_____

_____

_____

NOTES

Introduction

1. Mihaly Csikszentmihalyi, *Flow: The Psychology of Optimal Experience* (New York: HarperCollins, 2009), 95.

2. James K. Ambler et al., "Consensual BDSM Facilitates Role-Specific Altered States of Consciousness: A Preliminary Study," *Psychology of Consciousness: Theory, Research, and Practice* 4, no. 1 (2017): 75–91, https://doi.org/10.1037/cns0000097.

3. Emily N. Jamea, Leah A. McCaskill, and Rachel B. Needle, "Sexual Satisfaction: Exploring the Role of Flow," *Journal of Sex and Marital Therapy* 47, no. 5 (2021) 481–91.

4. Herbert Benson and William Proctor, *The Breakout Principle: How to Activate the Natural Trigger that Maximizes Creativity, Athletic Performance, Productivity, and Personal Well-Being* (New York: Scribner, 2003).

5. *Merriam-Webster*, s.v. "Eros (*n.*)," accessed 4/28/24, https://www.merriam-webster.com/dictionary/Eros.

1: The Indulgence of Sensuality

1. Jaqueline Fagard et al., "Fetal Origin of Sensorimotor Behavior," *Frontiers in Neurorobotics* 12, no. 23 (2018).

2. Katherine Harmon, "How Important Is Physical Contact with Your Infant?," *Scientific American*, May 6, 2010, https://www.scientificamerican.com/article/infant-touch/.

3. Alex Gibb, "Finding Happiness Is a Human Being, Not a Human Doing," TED video, April 30, 2021, https://www.ted.com/talks/alex_gibb_finding_happiness_is_a_human_being_not_a_human_doing.

4. "What Is Embodiment and Why Does It Matter?," YouTube video, 2:53, posted by the Embodiment Channel, August 1, 2013, https://www.youtube.com/watch?v=JYacDPOWsmE.

5. Mihaly Csikszentmihalyi, *Flow: The Psychology of Optimal Experience* (New York: HarperCollins, 2009), 95.

6. Gisela Telis, "Multitasking Splits the Brain," *Science*, April 15, 2010, https://www.science.org/content/article/multitasking-splits-the-brain.

7. Adam Gazzaley and Larry D. Rosen, *The Distracted Mind: Ancient Brains in a High-Tech World* (Cambridge, MA: MIT Press, 2016).

8. Sylvain Charron and Etienne Koechlin, "Divided Representation of Concurrent Goals in the Human Frontal Lobes," *Science* 28, no. 5976 (2010): 360–63, https://pubmed.ncbi.nlm.nih.gov/20395509/.

9. Gloria Mark, Victor M. Gonzalez, and Justin Harris, "No Task Left Behind? Examining the Nature of Fragmented Work," in *Proceedings of the SIGCHI Conference on Human Factors in Computing Systems (CHI '05)* (New York: Association for Computing Machinery, 2005), 321–30, https://doi.org/10.1145/1054972.1055017.

10. Gloria Mark, Stephen Voida, and Armand Cardello, "'A Pace Not Dictated by Electrons': An Empirical Study of Work Without Email," in *Proceedings of the SIGCHI Conference on Human Factors in Computing Systems (CHI '12)* (New York: Association for Computing Machinery, 2012), 555–64, https://doi.org/10.1145/2207676.2207754.

11. Ju Hwan Kim et al., "Possible Effects of Radiofrequency Electromagnetic Field Exposure on Central Nerve System," *Biomolecules & Therapeutics* 27, no. 3 (2019): 265–75.

12. Kevin P. Madore and Anthony D. Wagner, "Multicosts of Multitasking," *Cerebrum*, April 2019.

13. Emily Jamea, "The Role of Sensuality, Imagination, and Curiosity in High and Optimal Sexual Satisfaction," *Sexual and Relationship Therapy*, February 3, 2020, https://doi.org/10.1080/14681994.2020.1714023.

14. Elizabeth A. Babin. "An Examination of Predictors of Nonverbal and Verbal Communication of Pleasure during Sex and Sexual Satisfaction," *Journal of Social and Personal Relationships* 30, no 3 (2013): 265–75. https://doi.org/10.1177/0265407512454523.

15. "Lani Shiota: How Awe Transforms the Body and Mind," YouTube video, 34:22, posted by Greater Good Science Center, April 16, 2016, https://www.youtube.com/watch?v=uW8h3JIMmVQ.

16. Lori Brotto, *Better Sex through Mindfulness: How Women Can Cultivate Desire* (Vancouver, Canada: Greystone Books, 2018).

17. Peggy J. Kleinplatz and A. Dana Ménard, *Magnificent Sex: Lessons from Extraordinary Lovers* (New York: Routledge, 2020), 21, 107.

18. Beate Ditzen et al., "Effects of Different Kinds of Couple Interaction on Cortisol and Heart Rate Responses to Stress in Women," *Psychoneuroendocrinology* 32, no. 5 (2007): 565–74, https://doi.org/10.1016/j.psyneuen.2007.03.011; Chantal Triscoli et al., "Touch Between Romantic Partners: Being Stroked Is More

Pleasant Than Stroking and Decelerates Heart Rate," *Physiology and Behavior* 177 (August 2017): 169–75, doi: 10.1016/j.physbeh.2017.05.006.

19. Nicole Krauss, *The History of Love* (London: Viking, 2015), 73.

20. Healing sexual trauma isn't the primary focus of this book. If you're looking for literature on the effects of trauma on the body, a wonderful resource is *The Body Keeps the Score: Brain, Mind, and Body in the Healing of Trauma*, written by trauma expert Bessel van der Kolk, and *The Sexual Healing Journey: A Guide for Survivors of Sexual Abuse*, written by therapist and trauma expert Wendy Maltz.

21. Andrea Bradford and Cindy M. Meston, "The Impact of Anxiety on Sexual Arousal in Women," *Behaviour Research and Therapy* 44, no. 8 (2006): 1067–77, https://doi.org/10.1016/j.brat.2005.08.006.

22. Yael Ecker and Yoav Bar-Anan, "Conceptual Overlap Between Stimuli Increases Misattribution of Internal Experience," *Journal of Experimental Social Psychology* 83 (July 2019): 1–10, https://doi.org/10.1016/j.jesp.2019.03.006.

23. Tiffany Field, "Touch for Socioemotional and Physical Well-Being: A Review," *Developmental Review* 30, no. 4 (December 2010): 367–83, https://doi.org/10.1016/j.dr.2011.01.001.

24. Samantha A. Wagner et al., "Touch Me Just Enough: The Intersection of Adult Attachment, Intimate Touch, and Marital Satisfaction," *Journal of Social and Personal Relationships* 37, no. 6 (2020): 0265407520910791.

25. Anik Debrot et al., "Is Touch in Romantic Relationships Universally Beneficial for Psychological Well-Being? The Role of Attachment Avoidance," *Personality & Social Psychology Bulletin* 47, no. 10 (2021): 1495–509, https://doi.org/10.1177/0146167220977709.

26. Andrew K. Gulledge, Michelle H. Gulledge, and Robert F. Stahmann, "Romantic Physical Affection Types and Relationship Satisfaction," *American Journal of Family Therapy* 31, no. 4 (2003): 233–42.

27. Anik Debrot et al., "More Than Just Sex: Affection Mediates the Association Between Sexual Activity and Well-Being," *Personality & Social Psychology Bulletin* 43, no. 3 (2017): 287–99, https://doi.org/10.1177/0146167216684124.

28. Steven Kotler, *The Art of Impossible: A Peak Performance Primer* (New York: Harper Wave, 2021).

29. Kleinplatz and Ménard, *Magnificent Sex*.

30. Harold Leitenberg, Mark J. Detzer, and Debra Srebnik, "Gender Differences in Masturbation and the Relation of Masturbation Experience in Preadolescence and/or Early Adolescence to Sexual Behavior and Sexual Adjustment in Young Adulthood," *Archives of Sexual Behavior* 22 (April 1993): 87–98, https://doi.org/10.1007/BF01542359.

31. I am not at all opposed to the use of legal and ethical porn as an erotic stimulus. Using porn alone or with a partner can be a fun and healthy way to enhance sexual excitement. However, when the goal is to get more deeply in touch with the body, it is best to avoid any form of external stimulus.

32. Constance Avery-Clark, Linda Weiner, and Alexis Adams-Clark, "Sensate Focus for Sexual Concerns: An Updated, Critical Literature Review," *Current Sexual Health Reports* 11 (2019): 84–94.

33. Dale Purves et al., eds., "Mechanoreceptors Specialized to Receive Tactile Information" in *Neuroscience*, 2nd ed. (Sunderland, MA: Sinauer Associates, 2001), https://www.ncbi.nlm.nih.gov/books/NBK10895/.

2: The Excitement of Curiosity

1. Todd B. Kashdan et al., "The Curiosity and Exploration Inventory-II: Development, Factor Structure, and Psychometrics," *Journal of Research in Personality* 43, no. 6 (2009): 987–98, https://doi.org/10.1016/j.jrp.2009.04.011.

2. "Spencer Harrison, Jon Cohen: Curiosity Is Your Super Power," TED video, https://www.ted.com/talks/spencer_harrison_jon_cohen_curiosity_is_your _super_power.

3. Mary D. Salter Ainsworth and Silvia M. Bell, "Attachment, Exploration, and Separation: Illustrated by the Behavior of One-Year-Olds in a Strange Situation," *Child Development* 41, no. 1 (1970): 49–67, https://doi.org/10.2307/1127388; Leonid I. Perlovsky, Marie-Claude Bonniot-Cabanac, and Michael Cabanac de Lafregeyre, "Curiosity and Pleasure," 2010 International Joint Conference on Neural Networks (IJCNN), Barcelona, Spain, 2010, 1–3, doi: 10.1109/IJCNN.2010.5596867.

4. Lewis A. Douglas, Elena I. Varlinskaya, and Linda P. Spear, "Novel-Object Place Conditioning in Adolescent and Adult Male and Female Rats: Effects of Social Isolation," *Physiology & Behavior* 80, no. 2–3 (2003): 317–25, https://doi .org/10.1016/j.physbeh.2003.08.003.

5. Todd Kashdan, *Curious?: Discover the Missing Ingredient to a Fulfilling Life* (New York, Harper Perennial, 2010).

6. Paul J. Silvia, *Exploring the Psychology of Interest* (Oxford, England: Oxford University Press, 2006).

7. Emily Jamea, "The Role of Sensuality, Imagination, and Curiosity in High and Optimal Sexual Satisfaction," *Sexual and Relationship Therapy*, February 3, 2020, https://doi.org/10.1080/14681994.2020.1714023.

8. Rian Doris, "IntraConnected: Exploring Chaos and Rigidity in the Self with Dr. Dan Siegel (No. 121)," Flow Research Collective Radio podcast, March 20, 2023, https://www.flowresearchcollective.com/radio/intraconnected-exploring -chaos-and-rigidity-in-the-self-with-dr-dan-siegel.

9. Elizabeth Gilbert, *Eat, Pray, Love: One Woman's Search for Everything Across Italy, India, and Indonesia* (New York: Riverhead Books, 2017).

10. Peggy J. Kleinplatz and A. Dana Ménard, *Magnificent Sex: Lessons from Extraordinary Lovers* (New York: Routledge, 2020), 69.

11. Beatrice Rammstedt and Oliver P. John, "Big Five Inventory" in *Encyclopedia of Personality and Individual Differences*, ed. Virgil Zeigler-Hill and Todd K. Shackelford (Cham, Switzerland: Springer, 2020), https://doi.org/10.1007/978 -3-319-24612-3_445.

12. Todd B. Kashdan et al., "When Curiosity Breeds Intimacy: Taking Advantage of Intimacy Opportunities and Transforming Boring Conversations," *Journal of Personality* 79, no. 6 (2011): 1369–402, https://doi.org/10.1111/j.1467–6494.2010.00697.x.

13. John Mordechai Gottman and Nan Silver, *The Seven Principles for Making Marriage Work: A Practical Guide from the Country's Foremost Relationship Expert* (New York: Harmony Books, 2015).

14. Emily Jamea, "Sex & Islam (Episode # 17)," *Love & Libido* podcast, February 7, 2022, https://podcasts.apple.com/us/podcast/love-libido/id1572696112?i=1000550304426.

15. Carol Dweck, *Mindset: The New Psychology of Success* (New York: Ballantine, 2016).

16. Eli J. Finkel, *The All-or-Nothing Marriage: How the Best Marriages Work* (New York: Dutton, 2018).

17. Esther Perel, *Mating in Captivity: Unlocking Erotic Intelligence* (New York: Harper, 2007), 13.

18. Amy Muise et al., "Broadening Your Horizons: Self-Expanding Activities Promote Desire and Satisfaction in Established Romantic Relationships," *Journal of Personality and Social Psychology* 116, no. 2 (2019): 237–58, https://doi.org/10.1037/pspi0000148; Stephanie Raposo et al., "Self-Expansion Is Associated with Greater Relationship and Sexual Well-Being for Couples Coping with Low Sexual Desire," *Journal of Social and Personal Relationships* 37, no. 2 (2019): 602–23, https://doi.org/10.1177/0265407519875217.

19. Jamea, "The Role of Sensuality, Imagination, and Curiosity."

20. Kleinplatz and Ménard, *Magnificent Sex*, 49.

21. Jamea, "The Role of Sensuality, Imagination, and Curiosity"; Kleinplatz and Ménard, *Magnificent Sex*.

22. Visit my website, emilyjamea.com, for an online course devoted to reconnecting emotionally and sexually after having a baby.

23. Hazel J. Nichols et al., "Top Males Gain High Reproductive Success by Guarding More Successful Females in a Cooperatively Breeding Mongoose," *Animal Behaviour* 80, no. 4 (2010): 649–57, https://doi.org/10.1016/j.anbehav.2010.06.025.

24. Justin J. Lehmiller, *Tell Me What You Want: The Science of Sexual Desire and How It Can Help You Improve Your Sex Life* (Boston: Da Capo, 2018).

25. Some people struggle with unwanted sexual fantasies. These types of thoughts can create distress and disturbance. It's best to discuss any unwanted sexual thoughts with a certified sex therapist.

26. David A. Frederick et al., "What Keeps Passion Alive? Sexual Satisfaction Is Associated with Sexual Communication, Mood Setting, Sexual Variety, Oral Sex, Orgasm, and Sex Frequency in a National US Study," *Journal of Sex Research* 54, no. 2 (2017): 186–201, doi: 10.1080/00224499.2015.1137854.

27. Steven Kotler, *The Rise of Superman: Decoding the Science of Ultimate Human Performance* (Boston: New Harvest, 2014).

28. Amy C. Moors, "Five Misconceptions About Consensually Nonmonogamous Relationships," *Current Directions in Psychological Science* 32, no. 5 (2023): 355–61, https://doi.org/10.1177/09637214231166853. Amy C. Moors, William S. Ryan, and William J. Chopik, "Multiple Loves: The Effects of Attachment with Multiple Concurrent Romantic Partners on Relational Functioning," *Personality and Individual Differences* 147 (2019): 102–10.

29. From a marketing email sent on March 28, 2021.

30. Steven Kotler, *The Art of Impossible: A Peak Performance Primer* (New York: Harper Wave, 2021).

31. Frederick et al., "What Keeps Passion Alive?"

3: The Power of Adaptability

1. Michael T. Osborne et al., "Disentangling the Links Between Psychosocial Stress and Cardiovascular Disease," *Circulation: Cardiovascular Imaging* 13, no. 8 (2020): e010931, https://doi.org/10.1161/circimaging.120.010931; Ahmed Tawakol et al., "Relation Between Resting Amygdalar Activity and Cardiovascular Events: A Longitudinal and Cohort Study," *Lancet* 389, no. 10071 (2017): 834–45, https://doi.org/10.1016/S0140-6736(16)31714-7; G. David Batty et al., "Psychological Distress and Risk of Peripheral Vascular Disease, Abdominal Aortic Aneurysm, and Heart Failure: Pooling of Sixteen Cohort Studies," *Atherosclerosis* 236, no. 2 (2014): 385–88, https://doi.org/10.1016/j.atherosclerosis.2014.06.025; Hermann Nabi et al., "Increased Risk of Coronary Heart Disease Among Individuals Reporting Adverse Impact of Stress on Their Health: The Whitehall II Prospective Cohort Study," *European Heart Journal* 34, no. 34 (2013): 2697–705, https://doi.org/10.1093/eurheartj/eht216.

2. Jason Silva (@jasonsilva), "Desiring Intimacy Is Also a Desire for Healing, Instagram," April 30, 2023.

3. Susan A. David, *Emotional Agility: Get Unstuck, Embrace Change, and Thrive in Work and Life* (New York: Avery, 2016).

4. Viktor E. Frankl, *Man's Search for Meaning* (Boston, MA: Beacon Press, 2006).

5. Shanka Vedantam, "What We Gain from Pain," *Hidden Brain* podcast, July 4, 2022, https://hiddenbrain.org/podcast/what-we-gain-from-pain/.

6. Daniel Lim and David DeSteno, "Past Adversity Protects Against the Numeracy Bias in Compassion," *Emotion* 20, no. 8 (2020): 1344–56, https://doi.org/10.1037/emo0000655.

7. Erik G. Helzer and Eranda Jayawickreme, "Control and the 'Good Life,'" *Social Psychological and Personality Science* 6, no. 6 (2015): 653–60, https://doi.org/10.1177/1948550615576210.

8. Terry Real (@realterryreal), "Too Often, We Think Disharmony Spells the End of a Relationship. But Love Takes Work. I Always Say Intimacy Isn't," Instagram video, April 18, 2023, https://www.instagram.com/reel/CrMylXFNKvb/?img_index=1.

9. Bella DePaulo *The Lies We Tell and the Clues We Miss: Professional Papers* (CreateSpace Publishing, 2009).

10. Kyler R. Rasmussen et al., "Meta-analytic Connections Between Forgiveness and Health: The Moderating Effects of Forgiveness-Related Distinctions," *Psychology & Health* 34, no. 5 (2019): 515–34, https://doi.org/10.1080/08870446.2018.1545906.

11. Esther Perel, "The Secret to Desire in a Long-Term Relationship," TED video, 18:54, February 2013, https://www.ted.com/talks/esther_perel_the_secret_to_desire_in_a_long_term_relationship.

12. Mohammed M. Alsubaie et al., "The Role of Sources of Social Support on Depression and Quality of Life for University Students," *International Journal of Adolescence and Youth* 24, no. 4 (2019): 484–96, https://doi.org/10.1080/02673843.2019.1568887; Faith Ozbay et al., "Social Support and Resilience to Stress: From Neurobiology to Clinical Practice," *Psychiatry* 4, no. 5 (2007): 35–40; Yun-Hsuan Chang, Cheng-Ta Yang, and Shulan Hsieh, "Social Support Enhances the Mediating Effect of Psychological Resilience on the Relationship Between Life Satisfaction and Depressive Symptom Severity," *Scientific Reports* 13, no. 4818 (2023), https://doi.org/10.1038/s41598-023-31863-7.

13. "Jam, 2013, by Karen B. K. Chan," YouTube video, 5:52, posted by SexEd Project, January 31, 2013, https://www.youtube.com/watch?v=bgd3m-x46JU.

14. Akshita Uppot et al., "Responsiveness in the Face of Sexual Challenges: The Role of Sexual Growth and Destiny Beliefs," *Journal of Sex Research* 61, no. 1 (2023): 1–18, doi: 10.1080/00224499.2023.2175194.

15. Helen Singer Kaplan, *Disorders of Sexual Desire and Other New Concepts and Techniques in Sex Therapy* (New York: Simon & Schuster, 1979); R. Basson, "The Female Sexual Response: A Different Model," *Journal of Sex & Marital Therapy* 26, no. 1 (2000): 51–65, https://doi.org/10.1080/009262300278641; Emily Nagoski, *Come As You Are: The Surprising New Science That Will Transform Your Sex Life* (Melbourne: Scribe, 2015).

16. Nagoski, *Come As You Are.*

17. Peggy J. Kleinplatz and A. Dana Ménard, *Magnificent Sex: Lessons from Extraordinary Lovers* (New York: Routledge, 2020), 39.

18. Kleinplatz and Ménard, *Magnificent Sex.*

4: The Intensity of Vulnerability

1. Brené Brown, *The Gifts of Imperfection: Let Go of Who You Think You're Supposed to Be and Embrace Who You Are* (Center City, MN: Hazelden, 2010).

2. John Bowlby, *Attachment and Loss*, vol. 1. (New York: Basic Books, 1969), 194.

3. Mary D. Salter Ainsworth and Silvia M. Bell, "Attachment, Exploration, and Separation: Illustrated by the Behavior of One-Year-Olds in a Strange Situation," *Child Development* 41, no. 1 (1970), 49–67, https://doi.org/10.2307/1127388.

4. I am simplifying these styles. Disorganized Attachment is considered a fourth attachment style. It is the least common and most extreme style. It is characterized by components of both avoidant and anxious attachment styles.

5. Cindy Hazan and Phillip R. Shaver, "Romantic Love Conceptualized as an Attachment Process," *Journal of Personality and Social Psychology* 52, no. 3 (1987): 511–24, https://doi.org/10.1037/0022–3514.52.3.511.

6. Sue Johnson, *Hold Me Tight: Seven Conversations for a Lifetime of Love* (New York: Little, Brown Spark, 2008).

7. Pia Mellody, Andrea Wells Miller, and J. Keith Miller, *Facing Codependence: What It Is, Where It Comes from, How It Sabotages Our Lives* (San Francisco: HarperOne, 1989).

8. M. Scott Peck, *The Road Less Traveled: A New Psychology of Love, Traditional Values, and Spiritual Growth*, 25th ann. ed. (New York: Touchstone, 2003), 88–89, 93, 156.

9. C. G. Jung, *The Archetypes and the Collective Unconscious (Collected Works of C. G. Jung, vol. 9, part 1)*, (Princeton, NJ: Princeton University Press, 1981).

10. Richard C. Schwartz and Martha Sweezy, *Internal Family Systems Therapy*, 2nd ed. (New York: Guilford Press, 2019).

11. "Men, Intimacy & the "Right to Sex"—Between the Scenes," YouTube video, 5:10, posted by *The Daily Show*, October 19, 2022, https://www.youtube.com /watch?v=eYmFyjy2EmQ.

12. Kristin D. Neff, "Self-Compassion: Theory, Method, Research, and Intervention," *Annual Review of Psychology* 74 (2023): 193–218, https://doi.org/10.1146 /annurev-psych-032420–031047.

13. David Schnarch, *Passionate Marriage: Keeping Love and Intimacy Alive in Committed Relationships* (New York: W. W. Norton, 2009).

14. M. Scott Peck, *The Road Less Traveled*, 88–89, 93, 156.

15. "Becoming Irresistible: A New Model for Employee Engagement," Deloitte Insights, January 27, 2015, https://www2.deloitte.com/us/en/insights/deloitte -review/issue-16/employee-engagement-strategies.html/#endnote-sup-37.

16. Fergus P. Hughes, *Children, Play, and Development* (Los Angeles: SAGE, 2009).

17. Jeanette C. Lauer and Robert H. Lauer, *The Play Solution: How to Put the Fun and Excitement Back into Your Relationship* (Chicago: Contemporary Books, 2002); Krystyna S. Aune and Norman C. H. Wong, "Antecedents and Consequences of Adult Play in Romantic Relationships," *Personal Relationships* 9 (2002): 279–86.

18. René T. Proyer et al., "Adult Playfulness and Relationship Satisfaction: An APIM Analysis of Romantic Couples," *Journal of Research in Personality* 79 (April 2019): 40–48, https://doi.org/10.1016/j.jrp.2019.02.001.

19. Carol Bruess, "Why Play Is So Important in Relationships," Wit & Delight, July 27, 2021, https://witanddelight.com/2021/07/why-play-is-so-important-in -relationships/.

20. E. Sandra Byers, "Relationship Satisfaction and Sexual Satisfaction: A Longitudinal Study of Individuals in Long-Term Relationships," *Journal of Sex Research* 42, no. 2 (2005): 113–18, http://www.jstor.org/stable/3813147; Susan Sprecher, "Sexual Satisfaction in Premarital Relationships: Associations with Satisfaction, Love, Commitment, and Stability," *Journal of Sex Research* 39, no. 3 (2002): 190–96, http://www.jstor.org/stable/3813614; Amanda Londero-Santos, Jean Carlos Natividade, and Terezinha Féres-Carneiro, "Attachment and Relationship Satisfaction: Mediating Role of Perception of the Partner's Investment," *Journal of Relationships Research*, 11 (2020): E13, doi: 10.1017/jrr.2020.13.

21. Mihaly Csikszentmihalyi, *Flow: The Psychology of Optimal Experience* (New York: HarperCollins, 2009), 59.

22. Peggy J. Kleinplatz and A. Dana Ménard, *Magnificent Sex: Lessons from Extraordinary Lovers* (New York: Routledge, 2020), 161.

23. Hope Reese, "How Love Changes Your Brain," *New York Times*, April 15, 2022, https://www.nytimes.com/2022/04/15/well/mind/love-brain.html.

24. Steven Kotler, *The Art of Impossible: A Peak Performance Primer* (New York: Harper Wave, 2021.)

25. Robert H. Lustig, *The Hacking of the American Mind: The Science Behind the Corporate Takeover of Our Bodies and Brains* (New York: Penguin, 2017).

5: The Exhilaration of Attunement

1. Vittorio Gallese, "Mirror Neurons and Intentional Attunement: Commentary on Olds," *Journal of the American Psychoanalytic Association* 54, no. 1 (2006): 47–57.

2. Paul R. Amato et al., *Alone Together* (Cambridge, MA: Harvard University Press, 2007).

3. Ivan Norscia, Elisa Demuru, and Elisabetta Palagi, "She More Than He: Gender Bias Supports the Empathic Nature of Yawn Contagion in *Homo sapiens*," *Royal Society Open Science* 3 (February 2016): 150459, http://doi.org/10.1098/rsos.150459.

4. Marc H. Bornstein, Joan T. Suwalsky, and Dana A. Breakstone, "Emotional Relationships Between Mothers and Infants: Knowns, Unknowns, and Unknown Unknowns," *Development and Psychopathology* 24, no. 1 (2012): 113–23.

5. Tara M. Chaplin and Amelia Aldao, "Gender Differences in Emotion Expression in Children: A Meta-Analytic Review," *Psychological Bulletin* 139, no. 4 (2013): 735–65.

6. "Masculinity is mostly linked to insecure/dismissing attachment, whereas femininity is linked to insecure/fearful-preoccupied attachment"; Giacomo Ciocca et al., "Attachment Style, Sexual Orientation, and Biological Sex in their Relationships with Gender Role," *Journal of Sexual Medicine* 8, no. 1 (2019): 76–83; Chaplin and Aldao, "Gender Differences in Emotion Expression in Children."

7. For mental health crisis trends, visit the National Alliance on Mental Illness (nami.org).

8. Bridget K. Freihart and Cindy M. Meston, "Preliminary Evidence for a Relationship Between Physiological Synchrony and Sexual Satisfaction in Opposite-Sex Couples," *Journal of Sexual Medicine* 16, no. 12 (2019): 2000–10, https://doi.org/10.1016/j.jsxm.2019.09.023.

9. "John Gottman: How to Build Trust," YouTube video, 4:41, posted by Greater Good Science Center, October 28, 2011, https://www.youtube.com/watch?v=rgWnadSi91s&t=155s.

10. Richard V. Palumbo et al., "Interpersonal Autonomic Physiology: A Systematic Review of the Literature," *Personality and Social Psychology Review* 21, no. 2 (2017): 99–141, https://doi.org/10.1177/1088868316628405; Jonathan L. Helm, David A. Sbarra, and Emilio Ferrer, "Coregulation of Respiratory Sinus Arrhythmia in Adult Romantic Partners," *Emotion* 14, no. 3 (2014): 522–31, https://doi.org/10.1037/a0035960; Jonas Chatel-Goldman et al., "Touch Increases Autonomic Coupling Between Romantic Partners," *Frontiers in Behavioral Neuroscience* 8 (2014): article 95, https://doi.org/10.3389/fnbeh.2014.00095.

11. Freihart and Meston, "Preliminary Evidence for a Relationship."

12. Brandon Goleman, *Emotional Intelligence* (self-pub, 2019).

13. It is difficult to induce a flow state in a lab setting and even more difficult to understand the exact brain mechanisms at play. There are different theories about what happens in the brain, but the transient hypofrontality theory resonates the most with what my research participants described, which is why I chose to focus on this model. Clara Alameda, Daniel Sanabria, and Luis F. Ciria, "The Brain in Flow: A Systemic Review on the Neural Basis of the Flow State," *Cortex* 154 (September 2022): 348–64; Joshua Gold and Joseph Ciociari, "A Neurocognitive Model of Flow States and the Role of Cerebellar Internal Models," *Behavioural Brain Research* 407 (June 2021): 113244, doi: 10.1016/j.bbr.2021.113244; Arne Dietrich, "Neurocognitive Mechanisms Underlying the Experience of Flow," *Consciousness and Cognition* 13, no. 4 (2004): 746–61; Oliver Stoll and Jan M. Pithan, "Running and Flow: Does Controlled Running Lead to Flow-States? Testing the Transient Hypofrontality Theory" in *Flow Experience*, ed. László Harmat et al. (Cham, Switzerland: Springer, 2016).

14. Mihaly Csikszentmihalyi, *Flow: The Psychology of Optimal Experience* (New York: HarperCollins, 2009).

15. Rui M. Costa et al., "Altered States of Consciousness Are Related to Higher Sexual Responsiveness," *Consciousness and Cognition* 42 (May 2016): 135–41, https://doi.org/10.1016/j.concog.2016.03.013.

INDEX

ABOUT THE AUTHOR

DR. EMILY JAMEA is a sex and relationship therapist based in Houston, Texas. With over fifteen years of experience, she has helped thousands of people create connection and cultivate passion.

Emily offers online workshops as part of her mission to make her knowledge accessible to everyone. She speaks nationally and internationally to a diverse range of audiences, including educators, health professionals, executive and corporate groups, and the general public. Her expertise has been featured in *O, The Oprah Magazine*; CNN; *USA Today*; NBC; and more. Dr. Jamea hosts the popular *Love & Libido* podcast, writes columns for *Psychology Today* and *HealthyWomen*, and posts across all the social media channels @dremilyjamea.

In her free time, Emily enjoys spending time with her husband and children, traveling as much as possible, and salsa dancing and painting when she gets the chance.